I AM THE PEOPLE

RUTH BENEDICT BOOK SERIES

Edited by David Scott and Elizabeth A. Povinelli

Named after one of the founders of American anthropology and the Columbia Department of Anthropology, the Ruth Benedict Book Series is inspired by Benedict's passionate engagement with the critical political, aesthetic, and theoretical problems of the twentieth century but places them in the global conditions of the twenty-first. Contributions to the series explore contemporary critical thought in politics and aesthetics through a deep knowledge of the global condition in specific localities and regions. The scope of the series is capaciously theoretical and determinately international with special emphasis on settler-colonial, postcolonial, and capitalist regimes. The books present crisp interventions in a multiplicity of disciplines, but are also statements whose reckoning cuts across the critical humanistic and social sciences.

Secular Translations: Nation-State, Modern Self, and Calculative Reason, Talal Asad

I AM
THE PEOPLE

REFLECTIONS ON
POPULAR SOVEREIGNTY TODAY

PARTHA CHATTERJEE

COLUMBIA UNIVERSITY PRESS   *New York*

COLUMBIA UNIVERSITY PRESS

Publishers Since 1893

New York   Chichester, West Sussex

cup.columbia.edu

Copyright © 2020 Columbia University Press

Library of Congress Cataloging-in-Publication Data

Names: Caṭṭopādhyāẏa, Pārtha, author.

Title: I am the people : reflections on popular sovereignty today / Partha
Chatterjee.

Description: New York : Columbia University Press, [2020] | Series: Ruth
benedict book series | Includes bibliographical references and index.

Identifiers: LCCN 2019028666 (print) | LCCN 2019028667 (e-book) |
ISBN 9780231195485 (hardback) | ISBN 9780231195492
(trade paperback) | ISBN 9780231551359 (e-book)

Subjects: LCSH: Populism. | Liberalism. | Democracy. | Legitimacy of
governments. | Sovereignty. | World politics—1989–

Classification: LCC JC423 .C366 2020 (print) | LCC JC423 (e-book) |
DDC 320.56/62—dc23

LC record available at https://lccn.loc.gov/2019028666

LC e-book record available at https://lccn.loc.gov/2019028667

Columbia University Press books are printed on permanent and durable
acid-free paper.

Printed in the United States of America

Cover design: Chang Jae Lee

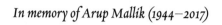

In memory of Arup Mallik (1944–2017)

CONTENTS

PREFACE

There is much discussion these days in the academy and in public forums on the threats that have suddenly appeared before Western liberal democracies. Since the end of World War II, these countries had enjoyed an unprecedented and unbroken spell of economic prosperity, social peace, and political legitimacy. Why is it that in the United States, Britain, and virtually every country in western Europe there is today, on the one hand, the rise of populist movements, authoritarian leaders, and a visible fragility of liberal institutions and, on the other, the failure of established political parties and representative governments to build consensus and maintain the legitimacy of the prevailing order? To many, the present situation has revived memories of the turmoil that ran through Europe in the period between the two world wars, ultimately plunging the whole world into the deadliest war in human history. Not surprisingly, there is urgent and deep concern in intellectual circles today on what should be done to preserve democratic institutions and liberal values from yet another menacing onslaught.

This book, based on the Ruth Benedict Lectures delivered at Columbia University in April 2018, points out the narrow provincialism of these discussions. Even though there is an awareness that advances made toward strengthening democratic institutions and practices in many parts of the world in the last decades of the twentieth century are now being reversed before our very eyes, the overwhelming theoretical concern seems to be with a set of pure and paradigmatic principles that are believed to be the hallmark of liberal representative democracy. This theoretical orthodoxy goes hand in hand with a less openly acknowledged prejudice that true democracy is the creation of Western civilization and that anything that goes by that name elsewhere, though it is always to be welcomed, is necessarily flawed or fake.

This book argues that, on the contrary, various features that are characteristic of democracies in Africa or Asia are now being seen in Europe and the United States because of underlying structural relations that have long tied metropolitan centers to their colonial and postcolonial peripheries. Historians are now showing, for instance, that the phenomenon of "liberalism at home, autocracy in the colonies" that long characterized European imperial politics was not a temporal lag to be ultimately corrected by the progress of some Whiggish clock of history. Rather, it was a necessary feature of liberalism itself—that is to say, liberal representative government at home required that there be authoritarian rule by expert bureaucrats in the colonies. Following the end of the old empires after World War II, a different set of structural conditions has emerged to tie together some two hundred formally sovereign nation-states in a new global order. This order is now characterized by networks of financial capital centralized in the United States and western Europe; giant U.S. technology corporations (now feebly challenged by one or two Chinese companies); the relocation of manufacturing industries in the emerging economies of Asia and Latin America; the rise of China as an economic superpower;

expanded international migration of laborers and refugees; and the waning of American economic influence alongside its unique status as the overwhelming military superpower. These changes, among others, have revealed in Western liberal democracies certain aspects of popular sovereignty that were hidden in its earlier history.

Contemporary populism in Europe and the United States will be much better understood if we turn our attention to its longer history in other parts of the world. Current academic studies of populism arose in the 1970s out of the analysis of Peronism in Argentina. Ernesto Laclau, in particular, attempted to show that, far from being a pathological infection threatening to destroy democracy, populism had its own rationality that was entirely consistent with democracy. Laclau's analysis led to much controversy, but it at least seemed to raise the debate beyond a sterile regurgitation of the age-old dogma of liberalism. Yet we now see that the predominant response to the so-called populist threat is an urgent call to defend existing institutions of government and law from the mindless assault of ignorant and resentful masses. Must democracy be saved by excising the people from it?

These lectures place the contemporary problems of democracy within a theoretically informed history of the universalization of the modern state on the grounds of popular sovereignty. Connected to this history is the coming to dominance of the bourgeoisie in the countries of North America and western Europe, the spread of European colonial rule in Africa and Asia, the rise of nationalism in the colonial world, the end of the European empires, the foundation of the welfare state and its subsequent slide into neoliberalism in the capitalist West, and the messy struggles with nation building and economic transformation in postcolonial countries. To carry out this gigantic analysis within the space of three lectures was an impossibly ambitious task. Fortunately, I was able to ride on the back of the theoretical work accomplished by Laclau, as well as his critics, and through that analytical window to explore the enormously rich historical and theoretical treasures in Antonio Gramsci's notebooks and Michel Foucault's lectures. I believe these were two of the greatest critics of capitalist democracy who nonetheless took liberalism with utmost seriousness. I have let them do much of the theoretical work for me.

Accordingly, I have argued that the travails of Western liberal democracy represent a crisis of the hegemony of the ruling order that in the last half century was based on what Gramsci called the integral state, in which the bourgeoisie, with the help of its allies, used the power of the state to influence institutions of civil society in order to educate the people to provide voluntary consent to its rule. Using Foucault, I argue that this was done mainly through the use of governmental power—on the one hand, to produce disciplined individuals as the normal citizen-subjects of the nation-state and, on the other, to regulate populations in the mass through biopolitical technologies. After passing through its liberal and neoliberal phases, this hegemonic order is now in shambles. What has appeared in the midst of various major and minor upheavals is a set of features— called tribalism, nepotism, cronyism, xenophobia, populism, etc.—that were hitherto regarded as belonging to the unenlightened zones of the contemporary world. I attempt to identify specific reasons why certain forms of postcolonial democratic practice are now raising their unseemly heads in the sacred lands of liberal democracy.

I have taken advantage of the colloquial style of the lecture format to meander through many geographical regions and historical periods without following any apparent topographical or chronological order. Nevertheless, there is a plan behind the idiosyncratic design of these lectures. They begin with chapter I, which focuses on a little-studied event in the inauguration of the new world order after World War II, when an Indian judge pronounced at the Tokyo war crimes trial of 1946–1948 that the victors of a war did not have the right to create new international law to punish the vanquished and that "even justice" required that every nation, including those under colonial rule, be recognized as having an equal right of sovereignty. This was an early sign of the tidal wave that would sweep across the colonial world in the decades that followed, giving birth to dozens of new nation-states in Africa, Asia, and the Caribbean. Many of them came into existence through bloody wars of liberation against the imperial powers, and many urged their citizens to continue to sacrifice to build their nations for future generations. How did the nation come to acquire this moral force?

To investigate this question, I turn to Johann Gottlieb Fichte's 1808 addresses to the German nation, in which he made a classic argument on the morality of nationalism. The true nation, Fichte claimed, was not merely an anthropological or constitutional fact; it had a spiritual existence that needed to be cultivated through education and the flourishing of a national culture built around its national language. Within this internal border the nation was always sovereign, even if it was under the political domination of a foreign power. Although Fichte was seldom acknowledged, this central moral claim of nationalism would resonate throughout the colonial world during the anti-imperialist struggles of the twentieth century.

Chapter 2 then investigates in detail the high point of modern liberal democracy in the welfare states of Europe. Through the 1949 lectures of the British sociologist T. H. Marshall, I show how hegemony was constructed within the integral state in which employment, housing, health care, and education were guaranteed by government to all citizens while consent was built through the mediation of political parties and trade unions.

I also identify the internal contradictions of this hegemonic order that would lead, as Foucault showed, to the neoliberal critique of the welfare state. A gulf was created between citizen-subjects as the bearers of rights and individual members of populations motivated by interests. Paradoxically, the very function of government as the overarching institution that took care of populations would create the need, even within the welfare state, for the optimal use of resources through technical administration by experts. The tactical management of interests would come to prevail over the guarantee of people's rights. Throughout the 1980s and 1990s, neoliberal governmental techniques would satisfy demands *differentially* (as Laclau terms it), tactically balancing the electoral heft of each particular interest against the constraint of resources. Ultimately, trade unions and ideologically coherent political parties were dismantled. Consent was now created by agreement among experts on the technical options available to government within given fiscal constraints. Parties tended to converge on policy matters, producing widespread apathy among voters.

This is the background against which a series of developments in the early years of the new millennium precipitated the crisis of hegemony. These include the 2001 attacks on the United States; the wars in Afghanistan, Iraq, Libya, and Syria; the global spread of terrorist violence by Islamist groups; the flood of migrants and refugees seeking to enter Europe; the financial crisis of 2008–2009; and the calamitous decline in the living standards of the less affluent and less educated sections of the people in the United States and western Europe. What is being called populism arose out of this toxic mix.

I have argued that this crisis of hegemony emanated from the tactical *contraction* of the integral state during the phase of neoliberal governmentality. The pedagogical function of eliciting consent from the governed, which had been carried out earlier through trade unions and political parties with mass following, was now consigned to the risky fortunes of the market. Instead of a moral sense of participation in sovereignty, the people were left with the mere empirical membership of a motley collection of population groups, each with specific interests and demands that would be met or denied in accordance with the technical determinations of policy. Soon successful populist movements and leaders would, as Laclau had suggested, rhetorically tie together the various unfulfilled demands of these heterogeneous populations into chains of equivalence, claiming that, despite all their differences, they constituted the authentic people who were facing a common enemy—namely, the oligarchy in power.

Yet discussions on populism in the West, whether they are liberal denunciations or hopeful approvals, remain superficial. Chapter 3 examines in detail the fifty-year history of populism in India to suggest that, unlike in Western liberal democracies, there has been in several postcolonial democracies a tactical *extension* of the state from the narrow confines of the propertied and largely urban middle classes to sections of the urban poor and the rural population—particularly those thrown out of traditional occupations and forced into the so-called informal sector. One aspect of populism in India consists of the distribution of targeted benefits to current and potential supporters, a form of governmental action not inconsistent with neoliberal techniques. Yet in an electoral democracy without strong ideological identification of voters with parties, there is every chance of a spiral of competitive populism in which rival parties announce more and more such benefits to woo voters. The other aspect of Indian populism is the ability of leaders and regimes to cope with changes in electoral conditions by rhetorically shifting the composition of "the people" and "the enemy." There are several populist parties in India that have maintained their electoral strength over decades and have often survived a change in leadership.

Even though populism has emerged in the West following a tactical contraction of the state, whereas in India it has resulted from its tactical extension, I argue that many features of Indian populism are likely to appear in the liberal democracies of the West. In particular, the possibility afforded to subaltern populations to anoint a sovereign of their choice who would fight the enemy and give them justice, without being bound by the opaque procedures of law and bureaucracy, is a powerful motivation that is likely to sway those people in Europe or the United States who feel disempowered by their invisible oligarchic rulers. What are likely to follow are features such as the centralization of power in the hands of an authoritarian leader, the repression of the opposition, the showering of benefits to a core base of supporters, and the undermining of institutional norms. Nevertheless, there will be the need to periodically renew the leader's mandate by defeating the opposition in popular elections.

What Indian populism also shows with compelling force is the effectiveness of visual representation in popular mobilization. Cinema and the melodramatic narrative form have had a direct influence on populist politics in India; this is not surprising in a country where most people do not read as a matter of habit. Liberal political theory, which has stubbornly refused to look beyond rational communication by means of textual discourse, would do well to take more seriously the autonomous power of visual and melodramatic communication in the age of President Donald Trump. What the history of populism in India strongly suggests is that once the electoral system enters a spiral of competitive populism, there is little chance of a simple return to liberal propriety.

Expanding on the original Ruth Benedict Lectures, the afterword to this book engages the question of what needs to be done to create conditions for a more meaningful participation of the people in sovereignty. I argue that proposals such as Chantal Mouffe's *For a Left Populism*, while correctly identifying the present moment as one laden with possibilities, ascribe a hegemonic drive to left-wing populism that is simply not there because populist politics is necessarily limited to tactical maneuvers; it cannot devise a strategy of social transformation. Such a counterhegemonic strategy would require, as Gramsci never tired of pointing out, social classes with the necessary consciousness and organization. As far as the capitalist countries of the West are concerned, there is at the present moment only one such fundamental class that is both organized and self-conscious of its historical mission—namely, the class of the owners of capital. To realize the truth of this statement one only needs to recall the speed and decisiveness with which the representatives of global finance, overcoming the many differences among them, mobilized the resources of their governments to tackle the financial crisis of 2008–2009. To suggest a genuine counterhegemonic strategy, we would first have to answer the question, Which social force is capable of formulating and carrying out such a strategy?

As far as countries like India are concerned, we are dealing with historical formations that are rather different. While corporate capital has established a hegemonic position in the urban civil society of the middle classes, its writ does not run among the rural population or those struggling to survive in the informal economy. A significant dilemma has appeared with the ruling Bharatiya Janata Party (BJP) taking power in 2014 under Prime Minister Narendra Modi with a promise to abandon the populist policies of earlier governments and bring in economic reforms that would create something like an integral state under capitalist hegemony. Yet the BJP also has a parallel hegemonic strategy of cultural transformation to establish

India as an essentially Hindu nation-state; such a strategy excludes minorities from the fold of the "authentic people" and marks Muslims, in particular, as threatening enemies. In the run-up to the elections of 2019, the former strategy has receded from view as electoral compulsions have forced Modi and the BJP to combine the age-old tactics of populist spending with the rhetoric of aggressive, indeed militarist, Hindu nationalism.

A counterhegemonic strategy, even if it is to build on the mobilization of popular energies that India's many populist leaders and parties have achieved, must necessarily step out of the confines of electoral tactics to forge new and more lasting pedagogical projects of social transformation that will ensure both justice and prosperity for the people. But here, too, the Gramscian question must be asked: Which social force will lead such a counterhegemonic project of transformation?

I am grateful to the Department of Anthropology at Columbia University for inviting me to deliver these lectures. In particular, I thank Nadia Abu El-Haj, Elizabeth Povinelli, and David Scott for their efforts in organizing the event and to Courtney Hooper for managing its logistics. I also thank Lila Abu-Lughod, David Scott, and Aarti Sethi for their generous introductions and Manan Ahmed for a provocative response. The discussion that followed each lecture was immensely productive; I must thank, in particular, Gil Anidjar, Tania Bhattacharya, Ayça Çubukçu, Mana Kia, Brian Larkin, Karuna Mantena, Uday Singh Mehta, Timothy Mitchell, Shayoni Mitra, and Sheldon Pollock for their questions and comments. I have also greatly benefited from the detailed comments I have received and discussions I have had with Talal Asad, Homi K. Bhabha, Akeel Bilgrami, Thomas Blom Hansen, Ira Katznelson, Mahmood Mamdani, Durba Mitra, and S. Akbar Zaidi.

I am grateful to the generous and immensely useful reviews commissioned by Columbia University Press on an earlier draft of this book. I also had the opportunity of presenting the contents of these lectures in a series of talks at the University of Bologna and the University Urbino Carlo Bo; I thank, in particular, Alessandro Avienzo, Paolo Capuzzo, Michele Filippini, Fabio Frosini, and Stefano Visentin for their comments. Finally, I express my thanks to Lowell Frye and Eric Schwartz of Columbia University Press for their care in seeing this book through the publication process and to Brian Bendlin for a superb job of copyediting. I thank Amron Gravett of Wild Clover Book Services for preparing the index.

New York
April 15, 2019

I AM THE PEOPLE

1

Even Justice

Guilty Nations

I was an undergraduate at Presidency College, Calcutta, in the mid-1960s when I first read Ruth Benedict's *The Chrysanthemum and the Sword*.[1] As far as I recall, the book came to the college's economics and politics library as a gift from the U.S. Information Service, the agency that performed, during the years of the Cold War, the task of disseminating among the literate classes of the Third World the virtues of American culture. I cannot now exactly recall the impression the book made on me; it probably left me quite confused. I remember being struck by the vivid description of what Benedict (1887–1948) claimed was the Japanese national character, whose traits appeared to me familiar and, at the same time, strange. I had, of course, seen the depiction of Japanese violence and cruelty in the Hollywood war movies that were a staple fare in the 1950s and 1960s. I was also aware that the Japanese had been on the verge of invading and occupying eastern India, that they had carried out a few bombing raids over Calcutta that had led to many panic-stricken families fleeing the city, and that the scorched-earth policy of the

British and their rush to forcibly procure food stocks for the garrisons had led in 1943 to one of the worst famines in modern history. All of these were still etched in the living memory of the city in which I grew up.[2] On the other hand, I had also been brought up on stories about Subhas Chandra Bose, who was ousted by Mohandas Karamchand Gandhi from his position of leadership in the Indian National Congress (INC), was repeatedly put in jail by the British, managed nonetheless to make a dramatic escape from India, unsuccessfully sought help from Adolf Hitler, and finally raised the Indian National Army (INA) in Japanese-occupied Malaya and Burma. Among the grown-ups around me, few believed that Bose had been killed in an air crash along with his Japanese allies as they hurriedly withdrew from Southeast Asia after Japan's surrender. Many harbored the thought that he was biding his time, waiting to make a triumphant return to his homeland. As I reached adulthood in the fervently anti-British years following India's independence, I did not think of the Japanese as a defeated enemy.

What I do remember quite clearly from my first reading of *The Chrysanthemum and the Sword* is my astonishment that Benedict—after confidently declaring that once Emperor Hirohito had announced Japan's surrender and urged his subjects to desist from further violence no Japanese would carry on the fight—did not once mention that the surrender had come only after the atomic bombs were dropped on Hiroshima and Nagasaki. I did not at the time know of the circumstances under which Benedict wrote the book, or indeed of who she was and how area specialists had been inducted into the American war effort. But in the mid-1960s, as my generation saw with increasing alarm and outrage the growing military involvement of the United States in Vietnam, this omission did not enhance in my estimation the credentials of the Columbia University anthropologist.

Reading the book today, one cannot help but be struck by the intellectual naïveté of an anthropological project seeking to identify a national personality for a large and complex society such as Japan. There was, of course, an external impetus. Benedict's work with the U.S. Office of War Information had led her to produce in the years 1943–1945 a series of reports on the "national character" of Danes, Finns, Norwegians, Romanians, and Thais.[3] Her study on Japan began in the same office, with Benedict deciding after World War II had ended to turn the material she had collected into a full-length book—one that she, according to her student Margaret Mead, cared more about than any of her other books.[4] By then she had developed the idea of national character studies into a fully formed method; in the last years of her life, she launched a major project, Columbia University Research in Contemporary Cultures, which was funded by the U.S. Office of Naval Research.[5] Indeed, this was part of a significant, if short-lived, trend in postwar American anthropology called culture and personality studies. Today, seventy years later, a critique of the assumptions underlying such a project would be obvious, and hence tedious. Here I want to focus instead on a specific character trait that Benedict emphasized in the Japanese personality.

There is a distinction to be made, she explains, between guilt cultures and shame cultures. In the former there are absolute standards of morality, and individuals are encouraged to develop a conscience of guilt. Immoral acts produce strong feelings of guilt in a person, who could then seek to find relief in confession or atonement. Needless to say, the culture of Protestant Christianity is an obvious example of such a guilt culture. Benedict goes on to say that in addition, persons in such societies might engage in bad or inappropriate behaviors that are not, however, sins against morality. Thus, in the United States, for instance, a person who is improperly dressed or says something inappropriate could feel chagrined, but this would not burden his or her conscience with guilt. Benedict argues that in a culture such as Japan's, where shame predominates, people feel ashamed about behavior for which Americans would simply feel guilty. The overwhelming social sanction that produces proper conduct in such societies is the intense feeling of public shame. Confession or atonement would not relieve such feelings. On the other hand, if the violation could be hidden from others, there need be no shame.[6]

Benedict draws out at length the implications of Japanese shame culture, and especially the duty to protect one's name, in a variety of situations that occur in families, educational institutions, professional life, politics, and warfare. The duty to protect one's name enjoins the Japanese to respond to insults with retaliation, to not admit any professional failure or ignorance, and to always observe the rules of behavior appropriate to one's station in life (116). Benedict explains how, given the powerful social sanction of shame, a person who feels defeated in his battle to vindicate his reputation will choose suicide as "a final argument to win victory." That is why so many Japanese soldiers chose certain death in battle instead of being taken prisoner (168). She also explains why, after the Japanese realized they had lost the war,

> they accepted the defeat and all its consequences with extreme good will. Americans were welcomed with bows and smiles, with handwavings and shouts of greeting. These people were not sullen nor angry. . . . The Japanese at the present moment are chiefly conscious of defending their good name in defeat and they feel they can do this by being friendly. As a corollary, many feel they can do it most safely by being dependent.
>
> (170–71)

I must note that while Benedict repeatedly points out the contrast between the cultural norms of the West (the United States, in particular) and those of Japan, she does not do so in a crude Orientalist fashion. She is well aware of the specific features of Japanese culture and how they differ from those of China, India, Indonesia, Thailand, and the Pacific islands. Benedict also notes, at various points, the cultural differences among various Western countries and how some of them may, in fact, be closer to Japanese norms than others. Even though she does emphasize the fundamental importance of hierarchy in Japanese culture and its contrast with the value put on equality in the United States, she does not, like Louis Dumont, for instance, elevate the difference to two opposed but universal normative paradigms of *Homo hierarchicus* and *Homo aequalis*.[7] Benedict stays close to her ethnographic material, avoids universal abstractions, and generalizes only at the level of what she calls the national character. If I am allowed to speculate a little, I think that at the end of World War II, with the United States thrust into a position of global leadership and the world poised on the brink of decolonization, Benedict was imagining humanity as a congeries of national peoples.

The explication of shame, and the corresponding virtues of duty, honor, loyalty, etc., occupy a large part of the text of *The Chrysanthemum and the Sword*. The opposite sentiment of guilt is described only in its manifestation as an inner feeling of individual conscience. Benedict does not dwell at all on the other aspect of guilt in Western cultures—namely, law and punishment. Guilt is not merely a matter of interiority; it also requires public discovery, proof, identification, and punishment. These are among the essential social instruments for ensuring conformity to norms and the deterrence of immoral conduct. With regard to postwar Japan, Benedict makes, in the last chapter of her book, an impassioned plea to the American authorities for

not adding further humiliation to the pain of defeat, for extending a generous helping hand toward economic reconstruction,
and for not attempting "to create by fiat a free, democratic Japan"
(314). She is skeptical about the usefulness of democratic
machineries such as popular elections and representative leg-
islatures, and suggests that it might be possible for Japan to
extend civil liberties and provide welfare to the people by suitably reinterpreting its traditional institutions rather than "on
the basis of Occidental ideology" (302–3). She does not mention that even as she was writing her book, preparations were
underway in the ruling circles in the United States to establish
by law the guilt of the Japanese in waging wars of aggression
against other people and to punish those among their erstwhile
rulers who were found guilty.

The Inconvenient Judge

The International Military Tribunal for the Far East was con-
vened in 1946 on the same principles as the Nuremberg trials,
with a few significant differences. In addition to ordinary war
crimes recognized in international law by virtue of the Hague
and Geneva Conventions, Nuremberg introduced two entirely
new concepts: crimes against peace (i.e., waging a war of aggression) and crimes against humanity (i.e., inhumane acts committed against civilian populations). After Japan's defeat, not
only were some 5,700 Japanese tried for conventional war crimes
and 920 executed, but also the decision was made to follow the
Nuremberg example and try the principal Japanese military and
political leaders for crimes against peace and against humanity.

There was no meeting such as the London Conference in
1945, where representatives of the four Allied powers drew up
the charter for the Nuremberg trials. Instead, General Douglas

MacArthur as supreme commander of the Allied forces in Japan decreed a charter for the Tokyo trials along the lines of the Nuremberg charter. A significant difference was that whereas at Nuremberg there were four judges representing the four Allied powers, it was decided that at Tokyo as many as eleven countries would be represented on the bench. The list is interesting. Besides the United States, which had been Japan's main adversary in the Pacific theater, and the Soviet Union, which entered the war against Japan at the very last stage, the three imperial powers whose colonial possessions had been seized by the Japanese (Britain, France, and the Netherlands) were represented. Australia and New Zealand, both British dominions whose mandated territories in the Pacific the Japanese had occupied, found seats on the bench. So did Canada, another British dominion. China, represented by the Kuomintang government, was the principal Asian country on the tribunal that had suffered Japanese aggression. Two last-minute additions were India and the Philippines. At British insistence, India was included as a country that had contributed numerous soldiers and huge resources to the war effort; besides, the Andaman and Nicobar Islands, a British Indian territory, had been occupied by the Japanese during the war. Even though India was on the verge of independence, in 1946 it was still under British rule. To further increase the representation of Asian countries that were victims of Japanese aggression, the Philippines was also brought on to the tribunal; that country had just established itself as an independent republic after Japan had withdrawn and the United States had relinquished its sovereignty claims.

The Tokyo trials began in May 1946 and lasted more than two years. The judgment was delivered in November 1948. Eight of the eleven judges concurred in finding all but two of the twenty-five accused guilty of conspiring to wage aggressive war; all twenty-five were found guilty of conventional war crimes.

Former Japanese prime ministers Tojo Hideki and Hirota Koki and five generals were sentenced to death. Three of the judges dissented: Henri Bernard of France disagreed with the decision not to indict the Japanese emperor; B. V. A. Röling of the Netherlands, while accepting that aggressive war was a crime, did not accept the reasoning offered by the other judges; and Radhabinod Pal of India absolved all of the accused of all charges. Significantly, a single judgment was delivered as the tribunal's finding and not as a majority judgment; the dissenting judgments were not published.[8]

Justice Pal explained his views in a set of public lectures at the University of Calcutta in 1951 and independently published his dissenting judgment in 1953.[9] Born in 1886 in a poor family in a village now in Bangladesh, Pal taught mathematics for a few years before entering the legal profession. He served as the officiating judge of the Calcutta High Court for two terms between 1941 and 1943.[10] By then he had established a reputation as a tax lawyer, a scholar of Hindu family law, and a professor at the university's law college. From 1944 to 1946 he held the prestigious position of vice chancellor of the University of Calcutta and apparently had a brush with Richard Casey, the governor of Bengal, who walked out of the university's annual convocation ceremony after being offended by certain politically inflected remarks in Pal's speech.[11] After the Tokyo trials, Pal came to be recognized as an expert on international law and was a member of the International Law Commission set up by the United Nations from 1954 until his death in 1966.

There is a story behind Pal's selection as the Indian judge on the Tokyo tribunal. When the War Department of the British Indian government was asked to recommend a name, it approached a few retired high court judges in India, all of whom refused, apparently because they were concerned about the politically predetermined nature of the trial. The War

Department then sought names of serving judges from the various high courts, and Pal expressed an interest. After his name was approved, doubts were raised about his suitability since he had been only an officiating judge. Yet by then the deed was done. It seems unlikely that the British authorities were aware of Pal's political views.[12]

In fact, it is clear from what is known about him that he did not have any explicit affiliation with any political party or leader. Ashis Nandy, who in 1990 wrote an essay on the significance of Pal's judgment and searched for his personal history, was unable to find anything more than a broad nationalist commitment, with perhaps a tinge of sympathy for anticolonial armed struggle typical among nationalists of his generation from Bengal.[13] Nariaki Nakazato, in an attempt to demystify the image created in Japan of Pal as an impartial and courageous defender of Japan's innocence in World War II, has since tried to piece together from sketchy and often speculative bits of evidence a story of Pal as a conservative anticommunist with strong sympathy for and even links with right-wing Hindu nationalism.[14] This tendentious account flies in the face of known facts, which suggest that Pal's political views as expressed in his judgment were utterly commonplace in Bengal in the 1940s. Japan's role in World War II was judged by most Indians alongside the history of the colonial occupation of Asian countries by British and other European powers. The INC refused to endorse the British war effort in World War II and, despite questions raised by some on the Left, launched a militant campaign against the British in August 1942, even as Japanese forces were poised on the eastern borders of India. The anti-British sentiments were magnified when Bose arrived in Singapore in October 1943 to take over leadership of the INA, which consisted of Indian soldiers captured by the Japanese and volunteers recruited from Indians in Malaya. There Bose set up the provisional government of Azad Hind, or Free India, under the protection of the Japanese.

This becomes significant because in 1945–1946, as preparations were on for the Tokyo trials, another set of court-martial proceedings were being carried out at the Red Fort in Delhi against senior officers of Bose's army who had been charged with waging war against the king-emperor. The INA trials were a sensation, causing mutinies in the Royal Indian Navy and unleashing a wave of popular support for the accused soldiers. Both the major Indian political parties—the Congress and the Muslim League, which were then engaged in intense and often bitter negotiations over independence—demanded the soldiers' release. Even a vocal and active antifascist campaigner like Jawaharlal Nehru, soon to be prime minister, bowed to the popular sentiment to put on his long-discarded barrister's robes and appear at the trial on the side of the defense. A year later, in a dramatic twist of historical irony, Nehru ended his famous "Tryst with Destiny" speech on August 15, 1947, with the salutation "Jai Hind," which Bose had introduced in the INA, subsequently turning it into the official greeting of the armed forces of independent India. The alleged traitors were recognized as national heroes when their convictions by court-martial were commuted. One of them, Shahnawaz Khan, was included in Nehru's cabinet in 1952 and went on to serve as a Congress minister for the next twenty-five years. Consequently, even if Pal nourished in his heart a streak of sympathy for the Japanese allies of Bose and his army, the sentiment was widely shared by Indians at the time.

It is also significant that after independence the Indian government never took a step to repudiate Pal's dissenting judgment, even though it may have caused some diplomatic embarrassment. Indeed, India did not attend the 1951 San Francisco conference at which a peace treaty was signed ending the

Allied occupation of Japan. Instead, India signed a separate peace treaty with Japan in 1952 in which it voluntarily waived the right to seek reparations for war damages. On the political front, Pal was asked by the ruling Congress Party in India to contest elections in 1953 for a seat in Parliament (he lost to a younger communist lawyer) and was bestowed with high national honors by the government. Ever since then his Tokyo judgment has been ritually commended by every Indian dignitary in the context of relations between India and Japan. It is important to point this out because, as I will argue, Pal's dissenting judgment carried the insignia of a particular moment in the transformation of the global order in the era of decolonization. That moment has now passed. To understand the historical significance of that moment, we must resist the temptation to employ our current common sense as the yardstick with which to judge Pal's position.

With that brief introduction to the person, I turn, as the counterpoint to Benedict's analysis, to Pal's views on the question of Japan's guilt.

"The World Is Not Ready"

Pal's judgment runs to 1,235 typed pages. A mimeographed copy in four volumes exists in the Rare Books and Manuscripts section of the Arthur W. Diamond Library at Columbia Law School. The length of the judgment is testimony to the effort the Indian judge put into making his reasoning as rigorous as possible. He undoubtedly knew that his views would be radically opposed to those of the other judges on the tribunal. Hence, he was keen to demonstrate that his findings were firmly based on existing legal scholarship, leading to what now appears as an excessive recourse to long quotations from Western jurists. But he also made clear that he had a completely different view of the structure of international power relations. What was this view?

Among the numerous legal points that Pal dealt with concerning the charges against the accused, I will discuss only those that pertain to what may be called national guilt.

First, Pal refused to accept that what was being characterized as aggressive war was criminal in international law as it existed before World War II. Reviewing the history of global diplomacy, he argued that prior to the 1928 Kellogg-Briand Pact, the idea of criminalizing war had not entered the field of international law. Even after the Kellogg-Briand pact supposedly outlawed aggressive war, several countries, including some of the Allied powers, had embarked on war outside their own national territories on the grounds that they were acts of self-defense. But, Pal pointed out, the Kellogg-Briand pact had left it to individual states to judge what actions the right of self-defense covered. As a result, the pact brought about no fundamental shift in the legal rights of a sovereign state to go to war in defense of its own security as determined by itself. Pal also did not accept that any generally shared customary practice had emerged in the international community that made aggressive war a crime. All that could be said was that there was a popular conviction that war was wrong, but this was not sufficient for a court to apply that aspiration as law. As Pal asserted, "When the conduct of nations is taken into account the law will perhaps be found to be *that only a lost war is a crime.*"[15]

Pal rejected the argument that the principles laid down at Nuremberg could be retroactively applied to acts committed several years earlier. The judges at Tokyo, he said, must act as a judicial tribunal and not an agency of power:

The so-called tribunal held according to the definition of crime *now* given by the victors obliterates the centuries of civilization which stretch between us and the summary slaying of the defeated in war. A trial with law thus prescribed will only be a sham employment of legal process for the satisfaction of a thirst for revenge. . . . Such a trial may justly create the feeling that the setting up of a tribunal . . . is much more a political than a legal affair, an essentially political objective having thus been cloaked by a judicial appearance.

(21)

Indeed, Pal went further in stating his fundamental objection to the way the tribunal was being used to create new law: "A victor nation is, under the international law, competent to set up a Tribunal for the trial of war criminals, but such a conqueror is not competent to legislate on international law" (35).

He also refused to accept the argument that the lack of a legal definition of "aggressive war" did not matter because the Nuremberg and Tokyo tribunals were supposedly being conducted on the basis of the general moral sense of humanity. It had been argued several times by the prosecution at Tokyo that even though it may be difficult to define what an aggressive war was, everyone knew that Germany and Japan had engaged in it. If this was the law, Pal argued, it would have no predictability, since the only eventuality in which that law could be enforced was the defeat of the aggressor, which was a risk that every party in war had to bear. Thus, such a law would not serve the purpose of deterring war. Further, outlawing war would impose an arbitrary freeze on the existing power relations between nations. Why should dominated nations be made to submit to eternal domination only in the name of peace? As Pal noted, "The part of humanity which has been lucky enough to enjoy political freedom can now well afford to have the deterministic ascetic outlook of life, and may think of peace in terms of political *status quo.* But every part of humanity has not been equally lucky and a considerable part is still haunted by the wishful thinking about escape from political domination" (117).

Second, Pal challenged the move to make "conspiracy" to wage war a crime under international law. The conspiracy charge was needed to make the entire senior leadership of Japan culpable for all the particular acts of war crime in which they were not always directly involved. The point was raised at Tokyo on behalf of the defense that the crime of conspiracy existed only in Anglo-American law and was unknown in the legal traditions of the other prosecuting nations. But Pal maintained that even if similar concepts were to be found in the domestic law of states, they were all designed to empower a sovereign state to preserve its own security. "There is no international superstate as yet," he explained. Hence, there did not exist any supranational sovereign entity against whose continued stability a criminal conspiracy might be defined (571).

Pal spent the largest part of his judgment—some seven hundred typewritten pages—analyzing the evidence on the alleged conspiracy hatched by the Japanese leaders, beginning with a political assassination in 1928, the occupation of Manchuria in 1931, the expansion into China beginning in 1937, the alliance with the Axis powers, the bombing of Pearl Harbor, and the overrunning of Southeast Asia. Once again he emphasized the necessary legal criterion: The question was not whether the Japanese actions were justified but whether they could be explained without the existence of a conspiracy (557). He proceeded to show that Japanese foreign policy and military actions were perfectly understandable in terms of standard practices adopted by sovereign states for their self-preservation. Thus, in the case of Japan, there were the perceived threats posed by the economic dominance of Britain, the diplomatic maneuvers of the United States, the spread of communism and Soviet influence, and the internal civil war and interventions of the other powers in China. It could, of course, be argued that there were specific designs behind specific policies carried out to achieve particular outcomes. But Pal refused to accept that there was a single criminal design behind the foreign policy pursued by Japan over more than a decade (560).[16] He noted that "the statesmen, diplomats and politicians of Japan were perhaps wrong, and perhaps they misled themselves. But they were not conspirators. They did not conspire" (558).

Pal also made an interesting contrast between Germany and Japan that touches on some of Benedict's observations. The prosecution had, of course, repeatedly made the case that Hitler's Germany and Hideki Tojo's Japan were fundamentally similar in the criminality of their internal and external policies. Pal, however, pointed out that unlike the trials held in Germany, the Tokyo trial did not see any of the Japanese witnesses complain that their people had been terrorized or enslaved by their leaders or that the latter acted out of any motive other than patriotism. Hitler's regime could have been accused of stifling the constitution and placing the state in opposition to society, but that could not be said of Japan, where the constitutional relation between state and society remained intact and unaffected by the war (698).[17] If it was argued that public opinion in Japan had been influenced by militarist propaganda and the social techniques of shaping human behavior, then such methods were "being utilized everywhere by every government. . . . If it is an evil, it is an evil of the day" (561).

In further explaining why the concept of conspiracy to wage aggressive war was invalid, Pal pointed out that both the Netherlands and the USSR had declared war on Japan before Japan had done so. Certainly it could not be argued that the Soviets were acting in self-defense: they declared war on Japan on August 9, 1945, three days after the atomic bomb was dropped on Hiroshima, at which point Japan was already a vanquished nation. Why was Japan being singled out for an offense that some of the prosecuting powers could be alleged to also have committed? (119–20). Pal insisted it was because the victorious side was now creating law on the basis of dubious definitions in order to suit its political interest. To the argument that a robber cannot be defended on the ground that every robber had not been punished, Pal had this to say: "This is certainly sound logic when we know for certain that robbery is a crime. When, however, we are still to determine whether or not a particular act in a particular community is or is not criminal, I believe it is a pertinent enquiry how the act in question stands in relation to the other members of the community and how the community looks upon the act when done by such other members" (120). In short, when the crime itself remains to be defined by the community as a whole, one set of accusers cannot invent a new law to punish the accused.

It is true that in absolving the top political and military leaders of Japan from the charge of responsibility for conventional war crimes carried out by Japanese officers and troops, Pal tended to diminish the value of the evidence offered before the tribunal. These are undoubtedly the weakest parts of his judgment. Even for such horrific incidents as the Nanjing Massacre, Pal seemed to endorse the defense counsel's plea that the evidence was exaggerated and unreliable. But he stated the legal ground for his conclusion in clear terms. He admitted that "the evidence is still overwhelming that atrocities were perpetrated by the members of the Japanese armed forces against the civilian population of some of the territories occupied by them as also against the prisoners of war" (609) and pointed out that hundreds of Japanese officers and troops had, in fact, been already tried and punished for such conventional war crimes. The question remained: Was there sufficient evidence to prove that the topmost political and military leaders of Japan were guilty of ordering or acquiescing in these crimes committed in the field? His answer was that "the evidence would not entitle us to infer that the members of the government in any way ordered, authorized or permitted the commission of these offenses. Nor can I accept the Prosecution hypothesis that such offenses were committed pursuant to any government policy" (629). Not restricting himself to this strictly legal view, Pal even suggested what could have been an appropriate *political* response to what was, in substance, a political and not a legal charge:

> The most ingenious of the reasons that were given for fixing the criminal responsibility on the accused is that thereby the character of the whole defeated nation will be amply vindicated, and this will help the promotion of better understanding and good feeling between the individual citizens of the defeated and of the victor states.... By the trial and punishment of these few persons who were really responsible for the war, the world will know that the defeated nation like all other nations was equally sinned against by these warlords.... If such is the object of a trial like the present, the same result could easily have been achieved by a commission of enquiry for war responsibility. Such a commission might have been manned by competent judges from different nationalities and their declaration would have produced the desired effect without any unnecessary straining of the law.
>
> (106–7)

The most egregious example of inhumane acts against civilian populations committed by the victorious side that was, needless to say, never subjected to international legal scrutiny was the dropping of the atomic bombs on Hiroshima and Nagasaki.

Pal referred to this several times in his judgment. He refused to accept the argument that the atomic bombs had prevented the killing of many more by shortening the war or that it had now united all of humanity in a feeling of shared destiny. His comment was acerbic: "But certainly such feelings were non-existent *at the time when* the bombs were dropped. I, for myself, do not perceive any such feeling of broad humanity in the justifying words of those who were responsible for their use. . . . I am not sure if the atom bombs have really succeeded in blowing away all the pre-war humbugs; we may be just dreaming" (66).[18] Pal referred to what Kaiser Wilhelm II of Germany was reported to have written to Kaiser Franz Joseph of Austria as soon as World War I began, that "everything must be put to fire and sword; men, women and children and old men must be slaughtered and not a tree or house must be left standing. With these methods of terrorism, which are alone capable of affecting a people as degenerate as the French, the war will be over in two months, whereas if I admit considerations of humanity it will be prolonged for years." Pal then remarked,

> In the Pacific war under our consideration, if there was anything approaching what is indicated in the above letter of the German Emperor, it is the decision coming from the allied powers to use the atom bomb. . . . If any indiscriminate destruction of civilian life and property is still illegitimate in warfare, then, in the Pacific war, this decision to use the atom bomb is the only near approach to the directives of the German Emperor during the first world war and of the Nazi leaders during the second world war. Nothing like this could be traced to the credit of the present accused.
>
> (620–21)

There are several stories told by his Japanese acquaintances about the deep impact left on Pal from his visit to Hiroshima in 1952.[19] We also know that every time he was offered honoraria or royalties for his lectures or publications in Japan, Pal asked that they be contributed to the fund for the Hiroshima Peace Memorial.[20]

After stating that he had found all of the accused not guilty of any of the charges and recommending that all of them be acquitted, Justice Pal concluded that it was dangerous to use a judicial tribunal to attain political objectives: "It has been said that a victor can dispense to the vanquished everything from mercy to vindictiveness, but the one thing the victor cannot give to the vanquished is justice. At least, if a tribunal be rooted in politics as opposed to law, no matter what its form and pretences, the apprehension thus expressed would be real, unless justice is really nothing else than the interests of the stronger" (700).[21] He then pointed to the danger lurking behind the conjuncture of postwar politics—namely, the reassertion of the old relations of world dominance:

> In times of trials and stress like those the international world is passing through, it is easy enough to mislead the people's mind by pointing to false causes as the fountain of all ills. . . . For those who want thus to control the popular mind, these are the opportune times; no other moment is more propitious for whispering into the popular ear the means of revenge while giving it the outward shape of the only solution demanded by the nature of the evils.[22]

It is certain that when writing these words, Pal was thinking not merely of the war crimes trial in Japan but the reoccupation of Burma and Malaya by the British, of Indonesia by the Dutch, of Indochina by the French, and perhaps even of the prosecution of the soldiers of the INA in British India.

From all that we know about him, not least from the research of Nariaki Nakazato, the most convincing description of the political position that framed Pal's judgment is that of a mainstream anti-imperialist nationalism that was beginning to be voiced in international forums by leaders from countries colonized by Western powers. His insistence that the accused at Tokyo be tried according to international law as it existed before the outbreak of the war, his upholding of the right of constitutionally legitimate leaders to protect the sovereignty of their nation, and his refusal to admit that the winning side in a war could make new law and apply it ex post facto were not, as some international law scholars have suggested, the results of a conservative ideology of legal positivism. In fact, debates on whether Pal's judgment was based on natural law assumptions or legal positivism miss a crucial anti-imperialist political move that was beginning to be made in the 1950s.[23] Pal was indeed turning legal positivism, a hallowed doctrine in the heyday of the European balance of power and imperialism, against the new attempt to stretch the definitions of the law to punish a defeated adversary in the name of humanity and reestablish an old order of domination. At the same time, he also invoked natural law concepts of universal freedom and equality to demand equal respect for the sovereign rights of every nation.

On later occasions, when he was not required to don the robes of a judge and pronounce the guilt or innocence of the accused, Pal was able to enunciate more clearly the political view that informed his theoretical position on international criminal law. In his lectures at the University of Calcutta in 1951, he described what happened in Asian countries after the end of the war. An independent republic was proclaimed in Indonesia immediately after the Japanese surrender in August 1945, "but it appears that the Dutch had previously been given signed assurances that they would be allowed to reassume domination of the East Indies as soon as they were reoccupied." Indeed, the occupying British forces started a war against Indonesian nationalists on behalf of the Dutch.[24] In a similar fashion, the French were allowed by the Allied powers to reoccupy Indochina. Korea, explained Pal,

> was crudely cut into two at the arbitrarily chosen line of the 38th parallel North latitude. . . . This was not merely partition. It was dismemberment. We hear so much of Southern Korea and Northern Korea. But we are not as yet told who decided on the partition, when and where, and how long this is going to last. All that the Koreans know is the Russians entered the country from the North and the Americans swept into it from the South and both stopped at the 38th parallel.
>
> (44)

This was, Pal remarked, a cynical modus vivendi resorted to by the Americans and Soviets, both of whom thought nothing of sacrificing Korean self-determination at the altar of power politics. His inference was stark: "The only conclusion one can draw from all these stories is that even now in the international world a people would get just as much freedom as it is strong enough to fight for and a dominating power would give the dominated people only as much freedom as it can be forced to yield" (52).

As a member of the International Law Commission, Pal was required in 1954 to vote on the Draft Code of Offences Against the Peace and Security of Mankind. His response was forthright: "In my view, at the present formative stage of the international community, *even justice* in matters contemplated in the draft is not possible" (vii; emphasis in original). His reasoning, once again, was that given the deeply uneven power relations between nations and the fact that most nations in the world were still under colonial domination, there could not be any expectation of justice: "In spite of all the laborious elaborateness and minuteness of the several provisions, any guilt under them would remain to be established and punished only by the outcome of a war" (viii). In other words, there was no possibility under the present formation of the international community to submit powerful nations to the rule of international criminal law; it would only be applied by the powerful against the weak. His advice was to wait for a more propitious historical moment. "When there is no possibility of even justice—and there is none and there cannot be any in the near future in the present case— the effort must wait. . . . Waiting, in the circumstances, may not altogether be futile. History does reveal the possibility of adjustment of interests without the intervention of any superior coercive force" (ix).

It is pertinent to remember that in 1954 most nations of the world did not have sovereignty. Africa was almost entirely under the colonial rule of Britain, France, and Portugal; many countries in Asia were still ruled by Britain and France, as were most countries in the Caribbean. The United Nations consisted of only fifty-nine members. Pal's position on the state of international power relations was loudly echoed at the Afro-Asian Conference in Bandung, Indonesia, in 1955. The slogan there was to carry forward the struggle for equal sovereign rights of all nations in the international community. Human rights were invoked *against* the dominant Western powers, who were accused of persisting in the practices of colonialism, racial discrimination, economic exploitation, and violence against weaker peoples.[25]

That moment is now buried in the past. Human rights are now invoked to impose sanctions, prosecute state functionaries, and sometimes carry out military interventions against countries in which the promise of national liberation has turned into the horrors of dictatorship, corruption, and civil strife. But it is significant that unlike Nuremberg, the Tokyo trial, with its glaring legal flaws, is barely remembered in the celebratory history of humanitarian intervention. The so-called crime against peace has disappeared from the lexicon of international diplomacy. It is not that wars have ended; it is just that states no longer declare war, in order to avoid being charged with the crime of aggression. Since World War II there have been only two countries that have declared war—India and Pakistan in their wars of 1965 and 1971.[26] Perhaps it was because the generals of the two armies at the time were once brother officers in the same British Indian army that they felt the need to bind themselves to the civilized code of gentlemanly warfare. For every other warring country, it appears that Pal's critique has been fully internalized. Instead of the hypocritical mask of legalism, there is now simply a cynical refusal to call an aggressive international military action an act of war. A confirmation of Pal's claim that even justice lies beyond our reach is the decision in April 2019 of the International Criminal Court in The Hague to abandon its plan to investigate the United States for war crimes in Afghanistan. Following noncooperation and threats from the superpower, including cancellation of the chief prosecutor's visa, the judges apparently decided to be "realistic" and not waste the court's resources in a case whose conclusions they would never be able to implement.[27]

It is not surprising that Pal's judgment, along with the Tokyo trial, has largely receded from public memory everywhere.[28] Only in Japan has he been turned by a resurgent, and often reactionary, nationalist upsurge into an icon of justice, the sole voice of protest against the wrongs done to the Japanese people by the victors of World War II. A monument was erected in 1997 for Pal in Kyoto at the Ryozen Gokoku shrine for the war dead, and in 2005 a memorial was built for him at the Yasukani Shrine in Tokyo that embodies in stone, image, ritual, and rhetoric the right-wing militarist narrative of modern Japanese history.[29] Pal is well remembered in Japan, even if for the wrong reasons.

To return to my positioning of Radhabinod Pal alongside, or against, Ruth Benedict, we might say that whereas for Benedict the world consisted of distinct nations with distinct cultural identities that could not, strictly speaking, be compared by any universal standards of morality, Pal was insisting that they be first recognized as having the same intrinsic rights of collective freedom and equality before they are subjected to the procedures of international justice. For Benedict, the diversity of national cultures, like the diversity of languages, was an anthropological fact. Hence, each nation had its own rules of morality defined by its culture. For Pal, the equal right of every nation to claim and defend its sovereignty was a universal principle of political morality, regardless of cultural difference. The two assertions were situated on different planes—Benedict's on that of national cultures and Pal's on that of nation-states—but in a world where the identity of national culture was fast becoming the universal ground for a claim to sovereign statehood, Benedict and Pal were pronouncing two quite different judgments on the politics of nationalism.

To understand the moral force of nationalism that swept across the colonized world of Africa, Asia, and the Caribbean in the years after World War II, I propose to now turn my attention to a different place and a different time—Germany under French occupation in 1808. Rest assured that I will soon return to present concerns.

The Moral Nation

With Berlin under the occupation of Napoleon's troops, the philosopher Johann Gottlieb Fichte (1762–1814) delivered fourteen addresses to the German nation in which he presented a new plan of national education that he urged all patriotic Germans to carry out.[30] In so doing he also enunciated a set of moral principles of nationalism that, whether or not it was acknowledged as coming from him, would powerfully resonate in many parts of the world for over a century and a half.

Fichte's depiction of the German people as possessing an original language developed in its original natural homeland has led to an easy characterization of his ideas as the source of German chauvinism and racism in the twentieth century. It is not difficult to read his addresses as a text of ethnic nationalism that celebrates the exclusive inherited identity of the German people over centuries. Against this it is also possible to read the same addresses as a text of linguistic nationalism that is in principle open to all who embrace the literary and cultural heritage of the German language.[31] I will return to these two alternative readings of Fichte in chapter 3; at the moment we do not have to resolve this debate in order to appreciate the emotional power of national loyalty that Fichte spoke of, no matter what the specific ground on which the identity of the nation with a people is established.

Fichte's understanding of the organic relation between language and nationality clearly owes much to Johann von Herder's claim that each nation possesses a unique culture built around its language. But Fichte gives it a distinct political content. To take his specific argument, Fichte believes that linguistic signs are not arbitrary but have natural origins. Therefore, since the German people have retained an original language that has developed in accordance with its natural power to creatively intervene in life, they are better able to develop their philosophy, science, and poetry by engaging directly with language as vital and sensuous matter than are the speakers of Romance languages who are imprisoned within the frame of Latin, a dead language. The cultivation of German as a living language—such as, most famously, in the Lutheran Reformation—created bonds between the educated and the unlettered that are quite different from the French Enlightenment, where the spirit of freedom, cut off from its natural roots in a living language, has resulted in the separation of irreligious and atheist philosophers from the mass of the people.

As Fichte asks in his "Eighth Address," "What is love of one's fatherland, or more properly: what is the love of the individual for his nation?"[32] It is a love that stems, Fichte notes, from the natural inclination of man "to find heaven on this earth, immersing it forever in his daily activity; anchoring it everlastingly in the temporal, and cultivating it . . . in a way visible to the mortal eye." Every noble spirit wants "to pay for his place on this earth and the short span allotted to him with something enduring, so that he as an individual, while not known to history . . . is conscious of leaving behind a public memorial to the fact that he also has been here." What is that place on earth where his life will endure beyond his death? Fichte answers, "Quite clearly, only an order of things that he could acknowledge as itself eternal and capable of receiving something eternal . . . the people from which he descends, among which he was educated and brought up, and through which he became what he is now" (96–97).

What is a people in the higher sense of the word? Fichte's answer is "the totality of men living with each other in society, constantly reproducing themselves spiritually and physically, the whole ruled by a particular development of the divine. It is the universality of this particular law that binds this throng into a natural, consistent whole, both in the eternal and temporal worlds" (98). The particular law that binds a particular people is universal. That is to say, each people that follows an original and natural course of development acquires a national character. Fichte asserts that "this law determines quite completely and perfectly what is called the national character of a people. . . . People who do not believe at all in originality and perpetual development but believe only in an eternal cycle of external life, and who become what they believe, are not a people in the higher sense at all, and since they are not in fact a people, they can have no national character" (98). The contrast with Benedict's concept of national character is stark. For Benedict, the national character of a people was an anthropological fact to be empirically explored and established. Fichte would have regarded that as a merely external phenomenon. A body of true people, he would have said, had to cultivate an inner spiritual life consistent with its original nature; only that could give it a national character that would command the moral obligation of noble men. "The divine has taken form in the people, and that which is original has seen fit to clothe it and set it forth in the world," Fichte explains, "and for this reason the divine will again emanate from it. The noble man, consequently, works for, sacrifices himself for, this people. . . . To save this nation he must even be prepared to die, so that it might live and he live in it the only life that he has ever wanted" (99).

Elaborating on the spiritual power of this feeling of love of the nation, Fichte argues that mere reason could never produce such an emotion: "It is not civic love of the constitution; for this love is not capable of such sacrifice if it remains simply a matter of reason. . . . It is only the promise of a life on earth outlasting this mortal life that inspires a love of fatherland unto death" (102). Alluding to the fact that Germans were under French occupation, Fichte goes on to claim that a German actually has dual citizenship—citizenship of the state in which he is born but also citizenship in the entire German nation, the common Fatherland united by the German language. The first—original and natural—frontiers of states are the internal frontiers, formed by the invisible bonds of common language. The outer demarcation of residence follows from the inner frontier: "It is not at all because men live among particular mountains and rivers that they are a people; rather they live together . . . because they are already a people."[33] Hence, the external fact that the German states were under foreign domination need not have prevented Germans from exercising their cultural sovereignty over the inner domain in which they had to carry out a new project of national education. They had to reject the lawless and divided world of the European powers—engaged in war, conquest, commerce, and balance of power—and continue on their own way as though they were alone. In an earlier work, as Isaac Nakhimovsky reminds us, Fichte had strongly argued for national economic independence and self-reliance as a guarantee for peace among nations.[34] With a thinly veiled reference to the latest world conqueror, Fichte said in his Thirteenth Address, "Let us leave it to foreigners to meet every new phenomenon with euphoria: to manufacture a new standard of greatness, to create new gods. . . . Our standard of greatness remains the old one: that only that is great that is capable of, and inspired by, ideas that bring only salvation to peoples; and let us leave judgment upon living men to the judgment of posterity."[35]

There is a debate among commentators on whether, by appealing to the nation as constituted by its internal frontiers, Fichte was advocating national education as a preparation for political resistance against the foreign occupation. Étienne Balibar has argued that instead one could read the inner borders as marking a space of refuge within which the cultural identity of a nation could develop without meeting any external political barriers.[36] One can find similar debates within nationalism in many countries where the Fichtean concept of the internal frontier made its appearance in the twentieth century. For instance, the early stirrings of nationalism in India under British rule were marked by the claim that whereas national progress in the external material fields of the economy, technology, and politics had to depend on learning from the West, in the inner spiritual domain of the family, language, and culture the nation was perennially sovereign; within that inner domain the nation had to act on its own, keeping out the colonial power.[37]

Nonetheless, as far as the emotive power of patriotic love is concerned, there is no doubt that Fichte's argument has held sway over that of rational political calculation. From Guiseppe Mazzini and Guiseppe Garibaldi in Italy to the Irish Republican Army, the message of armed struggle for national liberation reached the shores of India. Inspired by the call of patriotic duty, thousands of men and women took to politics, and some of them to arms, and were sent to prison; hundreds were executed. Even as decolonization took place in India through a negotiated and constitutional transfer of power, the sacrifices of martyred freedom fighters have been kept alive in popular memory, not so much by academic historians as by songs, poetry, drama, cinema, and the popular art of the streets and bazaars.

For all his labors with the intricacies of English legal prose, it would be surprising if Radhabinod Pal was not moved by some of this poetry of patriotic love. He was, after all, enunciating a radically new and powerful political sentiment on the international stage. The high ideal of patriotism and national purpose that Fichte had reserved for Germans, for him the true inheritors of the Reformation and the Enlightenment, Pal was now claiming on behalf of the nations of the East. Long infantilized and humiliated by the colonial powers, the peoples of Africa and Asia were perfectly capable, Pal declared, of reaching the highest levels of patriotic calling. Anticolonial nationalism was a worthy moral cause.

In chapter 2, I will turn to examine how, by the end of the twentieth century—and not just in India but all over the world—the morality of the nation came to be contaminated by the cynicism of power.

2

The Cynicism of Power

Delivering the inaugural Ruth Benedict Lectures in April 2017, Talal Asad, after launching a searing criticism of the arguments offered by contemporary liberal-secular philosophers in defense of the governmental practices pursued in North American and western European countries, asked whether the modern state is capable at all of responding to moral suasion, and if so, in what language. His answer was no, it is not; and if it is, it can respond only in the statistics-based language of calculative reason.[1] Here I propose to show that there is a history of the moral decline of the nation-state, that that decline had a paradoxical relation to the increased involvement of governments in taking care of larger and larger populations, and that the moral claims of the nation-state were frequently connected to the historical contingency of its relation to the people-nation.

Thus, even in the decades following World War II, when independent nation-states arose all over Africa, Asia, and the Caribbean, some through peaceful negotiation with imperial powers and others through violent wars of liberation, the capacity of these new states to exercise moral persuasion over the people was considerable. "Development" was the new national mission as postcolonial citizens were urged to forgo current consumption for the sake of the prosperity of future generations. It seemed as though Johann Gottlieb Fichte's rhetoric of sacrifice, which earlier had been used to mobilize people in the noble cause of freedom from colonial subjection, was now being expended by the new nation-state to garner support for the painful process of transforming the economy. By the last decades of the twentieth century, however, that capacity was virtually exhausted. How did that happen?

To answer this question I propose considering the writings of two European thinkers—one from the 1930s and the other from the 1970s. Antonio Gramsci (1891–1937), a prominent leader of the Italian Communist Party, filled eighteen notebooks as a prisoner in Benito Mussolini's Italy with extended reflections on the historical process of the formation of the people-nation as well as the nation-state (I will elaborate on the distinction later) in different European countries. Two concepts from Gramsci will be relevant for my discussion here: hegemony and passive revolution. But before I come to Gramsci, and to retain a connection with chapter 1, I wish to consider Michel Foucault's discussion of state sovereignty in his *"Society Must Be Defended": Lectures at the Collège de France, 1975–76.*[2]

The War Never Ended

As early as his preparatory lectures before *Discipline and Punish*, Michel Foucault(1926–1984) had made the striking claim that, contrary to Thomas Hobbes's famous theoretical demonstration, establishing an absolute sovereign through a social contract did not in fact bring the civil war as the war of groups against groups to an end. Rather, the civil war continued below the surface, as attested by the persistence of illegalities and frequent peasant and artisan revolts in the eighteenth and early nineteenth centuries. Indeed, politics became a continuation of the civil war.[3] In his 1976 lectures Foucault picks up the theme once more and develops, I think, a much more powerful argument about the continuation of war within a society that has been apparently pacified. Most notably, he does this through an examination of the rise of the modern disciplines of the human sciences, on the one hand, and historical discourse, on the other. As a result, Foucault brings us face-to-face with a set of challenges that we, as professional humanists or social scientists, are reluctant to recognize.

Thomas Hobbes's Leviathan was the absolute sovereign, the theoretical epitome of what Foucault described in *Discipline and Punish* as the classical form of sovereign power as a centralized repressive force.[4] The problem of the modern regime of power, however, parallels a shift in the locus of sovereignty from the absolute monarch to an abstract construct called the people. This historical transition in the ground of legitimate sovereignty is, I believe, often missed in our discussion of Foucault's study of power, and Foucault himself may be at fault for not emphasizing the point sufficiently. But in his second lecture in *"Society Must Be Defended"* Foucault says quite explicitly that "juridical systems, no matter whether they were theories or codes, allowed the democratization of sovereignty, and the establishment of a public right articulated with collective sovereignty, at the very time when [in the nineteenth century], to the extent that, and because the democratization of sovereignty was heavily ballasted by the mechanisms of disciplinary coercion."[5] Foucault's project is to explain how modern power can function as mechanisms of domination grounded in the sovereignty of the people while concealing domination behind the disciplinary forms of regulation and self-regulation.

To show us the stakes involved in this project, Foucault temporarily sets aside the abstract juridical-contractual concepts of political theory and focuses instead on the discourse of history, particularly in seventeenth-century England and eighteenth-century France. The writers of these histories held a variety of ideological orientations, from those of the radical Levellers and Diggers in England to the reactionary aristocrats in France. But they wrote the history, says Foucault, of the struggle between races—Normans against Saxons, Romans against Gauls, Gauls against Franks. Race here is most definitely not a sociological category. Foucault is at pains to explain that our modern-day understanding of *race* as a sociobiological term is only one particular meaning assumed by a word that, for his purposes of elucidating the discourse of history in Europe, must be understood in the more extended sense defined in the *Oxford English Dictionary* as "a group or class of people having some common feature."[6] Unlike Hobbes's description of the anarchic state of nature in which each person is at war with everyone else, the race struggle in history takes place where one group has, for the time being, asserted its dominance while the other group seeks to overthrow that domination. The war is between groups, collective entities called races—Normans, Saxons, Gauls, Franks. And it takes place below the surface of a system of laws made by the group that dominates the state. Foucault paraphrases: "Law is not pacification, for beneath the law, war continues to rage in all the mechanisms of power, even in the most regular. War is the motor behind institutions and order. In the smallest of its cogs, peace is waging a secret war."[7]

The crucial characteristic of this history of the race struggle is its contingency and indeterminacy, its irreducibly unpredictable character. Decisive outcomes are often the result of sheer accident. The historians show that the formation of great kingdoms are the result of invasion, conquest, usurpation, and assassination; victory and defeat in battle hinge on nothing more than exploiting an opportunity opened up by sheer chance. The lesson of this discourse of political history in the seventeenth or eighteenth century—and this is crucial for Foucault—is that there is no inherent moral legitimacy to the legally constituted state. It is simply the result of the temporary domination of one race over another; the subjugated race could, if it could seize the chance, overthrow the ruling power and establish its own dominance. These histories, therefore, do not proclaim any universal truth. They are partisan; they condemn the brutality and wickedness of those others who had overpowered or tricked the race into temporary subjugation. Even in defeat, they celebrate the bravery of one's own race and anticipate its future victory. They reject the continuous genealogies with older sovereignties that conquering regimes claim for themselves. In other words, the histories of race struggle challenge the unity that theories of sovereignty seek to build for a pacified society. Doggedly undermining the legitimacy of the established order of laws, they become a counterhistory of the state. Foucault notes that the specific meaning of the term *race* could assume many forms— defined, for instance, by a common language or religion. But everywhere the counterhistory would insist that two opposed groups are brought together within the unity of a polity only through the violent act of war.

From the seventeenth century onward, beginning with Hobbes's theory of sovereignty, the disciplines of knowledge that would become the human sciences tried assiduously to deny, or at least suppress, this bloody history of the formation of states. Foucault thinks Hobbes desperately wanted to reject the political use that was made in the civil wars of the historical knowledge of conquest, invasion, dispossession, confiscation, etc.: "Leviathan's invisible adversary is the Conquest." Foucault reads Hobbes as saying that "war or no war, defeat or no defeat, Conquest or covenant, it all comes down to the same thing. 'It's what you wanted, it is you, the subjects, who constituted the sovereignty that represents you.' The problem of the Conquest is therefore resolved."[8] In other words, theoretical knowledge comes to the rescue of the state threatened by the violent history of its own origins. The same relationship between the new disciplinary knowledges and the perennially disruptive discourse of history will be seen in the emergence of nation-states, the spread of colonial empires, and what Foucault calls internal colonialism.[9]

Based on my own study of British colonial history, I could give dozens of examples in which a theoretically grounded justification of the colonial state—framed within a certain universalist understanding, whether liberal or conservative, of the development of human societies—has attempted to tame the violent history of colonial conquest. Thus, Edmund Burke, conservative critic of the French Revolution, was also a ferocious opponent of the despotic misgovernment of Warren Hastings, the colonial governor of India. Hastings, he alleged, had scant regard for the ancient dynasties and laws of that civilized country. But when it came to the scandalous history of the British acquisition of Indian territories, the otherwise eloquent Burke was strangely reticent: "Many circumstances of this acquisition I pass by," he said in Parliament in 1788. "There is a secret veil to be drawn over the beginning of all governments. They had their origins, as the beginnings of all such things have had, in some matters that had as good be covered by obscurity."[10] And if I were to turn to a liberal, let me give you Thomas Babington Macaulay, the celebrated Whig historian of England, who wrote an essay in 1840 on Robert Clive, the founder of the empire in India. Macaulay could not deny the palpable evidence of the historical records that Clive, in his dealings with Oriental nobles, had descended to the lowest levels of Oriental trickery to secure his victory in battle. But historical judgment, noted Macaulay, must be relative. We must judge Clive not as his contemporaries judged him, but by the good consequences we see today as having resulted from his actions. Though still authoritarian and paternal, the state now sat far more lightly, securely, and happily on the people of India than at any time in its history. Therefore, suggested Macaulay, one must judge men like Clive with "a more than ordinary measure of indulgence."[11] Finally, if you prefer someone more philosophically rigorous than Macaulay, I could cite none other than Immanuel Kant, who said in his famous 1795 essay "Perpetual Peace" that although European conquests by war of overseas territories were unjust, the federation of nations must nevertheless accept the historical results of those conquests as naturally given and not attempt to resist them or undo the laws that Europeans had imposed on other peoples.[12]

The formation of the disciplines in the nineteenth century did have their effect on the historical discourse of race struggle. Theoretical knowledge successfully promulgated the truth that the consequences of historical processes were structurally irreversible. Rulers might be changed, and yesterday's downtrodden could stand up today and make themselves heard, but certain fundamental institutions produced by actual histories of violence and domination must nonetheless persist. European conquest and settlement of the Americas, the Atlantic slave trade, the primitive accumulation of capital, the dispossession of peasants and artisans, and colonial wars: they may all merit the severest moral condemnation, but the structural transformations they have wrought cannot be undone.

But if the old races—Normans, Saxons, Gauls, Franks, etc.— were no longer the constituent forces of historical struggle, what was the ground on which these fundamental institutions were to be founded? Foucault says that from the late eighteenth century onward, and especially in the nineteenth, there emerged a new subject of history: "It is what a historian of the period calls a 'society.' A society, but in the sense of an association, group, or body of individuals governed by a statute, a society made up of a certain number of individuals, and which has its own manners, customs, and even its own law. The something that begins to speak in history, that speaks of history, and of which history will speak, is what the vocabulary of the day called a 'nation.'"[13] In the eighteenth century, Foucault notes, this society-nation carried a sense such that the nobility was thought of as a nation, just as the bourgeoisie was also a nation.[14] But from the nineteenth century onward, as we know, the society-nation would acquire in Europe a more definite territorialized sense of the identity between people, nation, and state. Foucault claims that the earlier idea of nation would give rise in the nineteenth century to notions like nationality, race, and class.[15]

The new subject of history—society—brought about a methodological revolution in history writing. Instead of condemning the brutality or perfidy of the conquering race, historians began to seek the economic and political reasons for defeat. They discovered that instead of the natural equality of citizens as proclaimed by constitutional or juridical theory, what prevailed in actual history was the inequality produced by freedom. Instead of identifying and asserting public rights, therefore, historians began to see their field as the record of the interplay of the relation of social forces. They began to produce knowledge about nations, minorities, and classes. In fact, setting aside the juridical construction of the legal subject, the new history produced in the nineteenth century—now to be called social history—would adopt the state's administrative rationality (or *governmentality*—the word had not yet appeared in the Foucauldian lexicon in 1975) to construct its language of the historical analysis of social forces. By the twentieth century—through the invention of new methods of survey research and the deployment of a probabilistic rather than determinist form of scientific reasoning to bring under epistemic control a wide range of social phenomena conditioned by uncertainty—social history, like the other human sciences, would fully participate in the process of normalizing society.

For present purposes, I will summarize Foucault by suggesting that despite the formation of sovereign nation-states with laws and institutions to pacify and normalize society, the war continued on two planes. First, it continued to be waged between European states, but within a normative order of the law of nations, the balance of power and diplomatic civility. The key idea was that no power must be allowed to rise to dominate all of Europe. Toward this end, it was legitimate to forge alliances and go to war to contain a power that threatened to dominate. But as soon as that aim was achieved, the victorious allies were required, by the normative principles of balance-of-power diplomacy, to restore to the vanquished its territories and assets in order to return to a position of equitable balance; the loser was not to be punished for having waged war. To achieve this objective, European peace treaties in the eighteenth and nineteenth centuries frequently involved the seizure, partition, and exchange of the territories of lesser powers and colonial possessions in order to increase the size of the pie that was to be divided among the major powers. The most egregious examples of this technique in European diplomatic history are the three partitions of Poland in the late eighteenth century that obliterated that country as a sovereign state.[16]

Wars were also launched or sponsored by European states in other continents. There were three different ways in which these overseas conquests were normalized. In the Americas, or later in Australia and New Zealand, the vanquished indigenous peoples were considered so uncivilized as to be unworthy and incapable of inclusion in the political society of European settlers who would, in the late eighteenth and early nineteenth centuries, launch the first national revolutions in the colonial world and set up modern republican states for themselves. Over time, through unequal treaties and exclusion policies, those Native Americans who survived were allowed certain zones of supervised autonomy in which they largely languished in poverty and hopelessness. In other European colonies in the Americas and the Caribbean, large plantations owned by settlers were put to profitable production by importing African slave labor. After the abolition of slavery, the labor force in Caribbean colonies was supplied by indentured laborers from Asia. But when Europeans came to acquire territories in Asia in the eighteenth century, they were confronted by dense agrarian societies with flourishing manufacturing trades and sophisticated institutions of bureaucracy and law. Even as European powers established their military superiority over local sovereigns, the conquest had to be legitimized in a way that included native elites as collaborators and native populations as pacified subjects. This resulted not in the extension of the European law of nations to Asian partners but rather in a system of subordinate, partial, and graded sovereignties operated not by law but by policy.[17] The same framework of inferior sovereignties was applied later to Africa when it was conquered by and divided up between European imperial powers, the policy coming to acquire the name *indirect rule*.[18] In some of these cases, subordinate sovereignty was merely a device to ensure extraction of resources without intervening in domestic society, whereas in others it led to the colonial creation of so-called customary law administered by tribal chiefs to maintain order in the countryside and supply docile labor to colonial towns and plantations. In all of these instances, the violent and contingent history of colonial conquest was concealed by a normative discourse of social pacification, commerce, and universal progress. Further, the concept of uniquely defined territorial sovereignty was exported to the colonial world because of the requirements of the European balance of power. Overseas colonial possessions had to be cartographically demarcated in order to define and stabilize relations among European powers, not because African or Asian sovereigns were included within the family of nations.

The second plane on which the war continued was that of the supposedly pacified and constitutionally normalized domestic terrain of the sovereign nation-state in the Americas or Europe. As Foucault suggests, it was no longer a race struggle of the old kind but rather the perceived dominance of one group, defined by language, religion, ethnicity, region, or class, that would be accused of imposing the peace on its terms over the others. And since sovereignty in the nation-state was supposed to be derived from the people, politics—especially democratic politics— would come to be defined by the conflict of social groups claiming their just shares within the institutions of the state.

It is in the latter theater of the war among social groups to achieve dominance over the people-nation that I find Gramsci's writings particularly perceptive in explaining to us how, through wars of maneuver and position, fundamental social classes struggled with one another to structure in their favor the relations between state and society. Gramsci, I believe, is particularly useful in understanding how the contingent, accidental, partisan, and often fortuitous history of political battles is transformed into the universalist legal and constitutional discourse of freedom and equality. The former, in Gramsci, is the history of passive revolution; the latter is hegemony.

The Elusive Ethical State

Gramsci's acknowledgment of the innate unpredictability of historical events can be found as early as his short article greeting the October Revolution. Calling it "the revolution against Karl Marx's *Capital*," Gramsci described the revolution in Russia as the rebuttal by history of the structural predictions of Marx's analysis of capital: "Events have exploded the critical schema determining how the history of Russia would unfold according to the canons of historical materialism. The Bolsheviks reject Karl Marx." This startling announcement is followed by an insistent distinction between normal conditions of history and a sudden, unexpected, and intensified sequence of events that can galvanize the will of the people:

> *In normal times* a lengthy process of gradual diffusion through society is needed for such a collective will to form. . . . That is why, *under normal conditions*, the canons of Marxist historical criticism grasp reality, capture and clarify it. . . . But in Russia the war galvanized the people's will. As a result of the sufferings accumulated over three years, their will became one almost overnight. . . . Socialist propaganda could bring the history of the proletariat dramatically to life in a moment. . . . Why should they wait for the history of England to be repeated in Russia, for the bourgeoisie to arise, for the class struggle to begin, so that class consciousness may be formed . . . ? The Russian people—or at least a minority of the Russian people—has already passed through these experiences in thought.[19]

Even though Gramsci's characterization in the same article of the Russian Revolution as "the spontaneous expression of a *biological* necessity" seems to muddle the point somewhat, one can nevertheless hear an unmistakable echo of Foucault's distinction between the normalized order of disciplinary thought and the unpredictable contingency of historical events. Indeed, even though Gramsci's arguments would become far more nuanced over the two subsequent decades, the perpetually fraught relation between a theoretically unified conceptualization of the social formation and the accidental unfolding of actual history seems to haunt his thought. Gramsci tries to analyze that tangled relation by setting up what I would call a theoretical model of the Jacobin revolution and comparing against that standard the actual histories in each of the major European countries of the coming to power of the bourgeoisie. In the course of that exercise he sets up, I argue, a distinction between the historical formation of the nation-state and that of the people-nation. These two distinct histories are bound together by an aspiring ruling bloc with the help of a hegemonic ideology and the politics of passive revolution.

For Gramsci, the Jacobins represented an energetic organized force that pushed the French bourgeoisie forward, "leading it to a much more advanced position than it would have 'spontaneously' wanted and even much more advanced than the historical premises would have allowed." The whole French Revolution is thus characterized by the actions of the Jacobins, who "force the situation and produce irreversible *faits accomplis*, pushing the bourgeois class forward with kicks in the backside."[20] The result was the creation of a nation-state that made no compromises with the old governing classes, allowed no intermediate halting stations, and sent to the guillotine not only the representatives of the nobility but also yesterday's revolutionaries who tried to slow down the pace of change. As Gramsci notes,

The Jacobins, then, represent the only party of the revolution in that they not only perceive the immediate interests of the actual physical individuals who constitute the
French bourgeoisie, but they also perceive the interests of
tomorrow and not just those of particular physical individuals, but of the other social strata of the third estate which
tomorrow will become bourgeois, because they are convinced of *égalité* and *fraternité*.[21]

Thus, the Jacobins "not only founded the bourgeois state
and made of the bourgeoisie the 'dominant' class, but they did
more ..., they made of the bourgeoisie the leading hegemonic
class, that is, they provided the state with a permanent home."[22]

Drawing upon this historic achievement of the French Revolution, G. W. F. Hegel formulated, says Gramsci, the idealist
conception of the ethical state in which civil society is an autonomous domain of private interests and government is by consent of the governed. State and civil society are thus perfectly
balanced and force does not outweigh consent: "The state has
and demands consent, but it also 'educates' this consent through
political and trade-union associations which, however, are private organizations, left to the private initiative of the ruling
class." Hegel's ethical state, therefore, "already goes beyond pure
constitutionalism and theorizes the parliamentary state with its
regime of parties."[23] But then, in a move resembling a twentieth-
century update of the young Marx's critique of Hegel's theory
of the state, Gramsci immediately unmasks the real political
form of the ideal ethical state:

The "normal" exercise of hegemony on the now classic terrain of the parliamentary regime ... appears to be backed
by the consent of the majority, expressed by the so-called
organs of public opinion (which in certain situations,

therefore, are artificially multiplied). Between force and consent stands corruption—fraud (which is characteristic of certain situations in which it is difficult to exercise the hegemonic function while the use of force presents too many dangers); that is, the procurement of the antagonist's ... debilitation and paralysis by buying (covertly under normal circumstances, openly in the case of anticipated danger) their leaders in order to create confusion and disorder among the antagonist ranks.[24]

The political exercise of bourgeois hegemony in the real history of modern European nations cannot, therefore, be studied in terms of the standard of the ethical state.[25] What is required is an understanding of the nation-state produced through passive revolution.

Passive Revolution and the Integral State

Gramsci defines, expands, and deploys the concept of passive revolution in several notebook entries between 1930 and 1935. He uses it mainly to describe the formation of nation-states in Europe, including in particular the Italian Risorgimento, in which the radical Jacobin element was missing. The process was thus characterized by elements of revolution as well as restoration,

in which the demands which in France found a Jacobin-Napoleonic expression were satisfied by small doses, legally, in a reformist manner—in such a way that it was possible to preserve the political and economic position of the old feudal classes, to avoid agrarian reform, and, especially, to avoid the popular masses going through a period of

political experience such as occurred in France in the years
of Jacobinism, in 1831, and in 1848.[26]

The Risorgimento was a typical case of passive revolution. Even
though it achieved the territorial unification and international
recognition of the sovereignty of the nation-state, there was no
consolidation or politico-cultural expression of a national popular consciousness. What won in the end was the decisive quality of the leadership of the Moderate Party, which was aware not
only of its own political objectives but also of the limitations of
the more radical Action Party. The extent of bourgeois hegemony over the new Italian nation-state was determined by the
accidental outcomes of actual historical conflicts.

In contrast with the separation of civil society and state in the
ideal ethical state, the integral state produced by passive revolution unifies the two without dissolving them and produces a new
state formation in which state agencies (or governmental organs)
assume the role of educators of society. Thus, the bourgeoisie
exercises its leadership over other classes through a complex
hegemonic strategy combining activities in the economic and
cultural sphere of civil society with those in the legal and political sphere of the state. Gramsci's comparisons of the different
historical trajectories of bourgeois ascendancy in the countries
of western Europe, recorded in various entries in several notebooks, suggest that he was convinced that passive revolution
within an integral state was indeed the general form of continued innovations in the ruling strategies of the bourgeoisie—
strategies that are best described in metaphors of war (i.e., war
of position and war of maneuver).

Passive revolution involves an attempt by a ruling bloc, consisting of parties and leaders representing several classes with
varying degrees of power within the bloc, to pull together two

different histories—one of the nation-state and the other of the people-nation—that do not necessarily move in step. Gramsci's elaborate remarks on Italian history make it clear that, in his own country, the nation-state was formed first when the people-nation had not taken shape at all. Key here is the role of intellectuals. In Italy, intellectuals continued to work in the Renaissance mode, embellishing a high culture that had long gone sterile. In Germany, on the other hand (and here we can hardly miss the resonance with the observations of Fichte that I recounted in chapter 1), the Lutheran Reformation and Calvinism created the solid foundation for a popular culture in the Protestant nations; only later did German intellectuals produce a high culture combining the Reformation with the lessons of the French Revolution. In other words, the history of the people-nation in Germany was in advance of that of the nation-state. "Because of its popular development," notes Gramsci, "the Reformation was able to resist the armed assault of the Catholic coalition, and thus the German nation [here, meaning the nation-state] was founded."[27] In Russia, active and enterprising members of the elite went abroad to absorb the culture of the most advanced Western countries, but returned to renew sentimental and historical ties with their own people. The Russian awakening in the nineteenth century had an essentially national-popular character. By contrast, the old class of English landowners, even as it lost its economic dominance to the rising bourgeoisie, retained for a long time its political and intellectual supremacy: "The old landed class is joined to the industrialists by a kind of suture similar to the one by which in other countries the dominant classes are joined to the 'traditional intellectuals.'"[28]

Passive revolution takes variable forms because the actual history of nation-state formation and the degree of popular mobilization follow unpredictable trajectories that, although conditioned by underlying social forces, are pushed forward by the decisive strategic action of parties, leaders, and movements. Such action, Gramsci explains, involves varying combinations of trench warfare to defend fortified bases of class power in various social and political institutions, a prolonged strategy of attrition and molecular change (the war of position), and a frontal assault on the citadels of state power (the war of maneuver). Hegemony is complexly structured, with the domination and leadership of the bourgeoisie variably distributed over allied and antagonist classes, as well as over different institutional sites of political, economic, and cultural power.

Did the nation-states of Europe command the loyalty and affection of their people? We know that the second half of the nineteenth century saw a wave of movements by linguistic nationalities in Europe. They demanded, and often gained, their own states, thus shaking the foundations of the old multiethnic and multilingual continental empires. The idea of popular sovereignty proclaimed by the republican revolutions in the settler colonies of the Americas and in France swept across Europe to produce an entirely novel set of political identities, with people equaling nation and nation equaling state. Alongside and in response to these democratic revolutions (in which the working classes took an active part), the states of Europe strengthened their representative institutions, expanding suffrage to include large sections of working-class men. Perhaps most significantly, these states greatly expanded primary and secondary education in the standardized national language and mobilized most adult men into their national armies. Warfare among European states became more frequent, more destructive, and more national. By the turn of the twentieth century the international organization of the European working classes was at its strongest, but it was unable to resist the social democratic parties and trade unions from endorsing the war efforts of their respective nation-states. When World War I broke out and the states of Europe asked for the ultimate sacrifice from their people, they were not turned away.

After twenty million people had perished in the deadliest war in history, U.S. president Woodrow Wilson and Soviet premier Vladimir Lenin both declared, even if from completely opposed political positions, the right of nations to self-determination. Though Wilson meant that right to apply only to the European provinces of the Habsburg and Ottoman Empires, and the slogan provided some ideological cover for white settler colonies such as Australia, Canada, New Zealand, and South Africa to claim a democratic basis to perpetuate their rule over indigenous peoples,[29] the call for national self-determination would resonate loudly in subsequent decades in the colonized countries of Africa, Asia, and the Caribbean. We should not be surprised, therefore, by the position that Justice Radhabinod Pal took at the end of World War II when he demanded equal respect for the sovereignty claims of every nation seeking its own independent state. The same demand would be made by the political leaders of the countries of Africa and Asia at the Bandung Conference in 1955, when formal decolonization was under way but by no means completed.

When and how did the moral claims of the nation-state fade? To answer this question we have to trace the process of reorganization of the integral state in advanced capitalist economies in the second half of the twentieth century—a process that led to the severing of the affective bond between the people-nation and the nation-state. The state could no longer call upon the people to sacrifice their lives in the interest of the nation.

Liberal Governmentality and Biopolitics

An indication of how the relation between the state and the people was changing can be found in the report presented to the British Parliament by the economist William Beveridge in November 1942, in the middle of World War II.[30] It offered to the British people a comprehensive plan through which, in return for the hardships and sacrifices they were enduring, they were promised to be provided after the war with state-sponsored benefits that would do away with the five great evils of modern society: want, disease, ignorance, squalor, and idleness. Beveridge emphasized the importance of beginning anew by pointing out that his plan for social insurance aimed at universal coverage and was not "restricted by consideration of sectional interests," adding somewhat grandiloquently, "Now, when the war is abolishing landmarks of every kind, is the opportunity for using experience in a clear field. A revolutionary moment in the world's history is a time for revolutions, not for patching." He also clarified that in providing social security, the state would not stifle incentive, opportunity, or responsibility: "In establishing a national minimum, it should leave room and encouragement for voluntary action by each individual to provide more than that minimum for himself and his family."[31]

Even though Prime Minister Winston Churchill and most of the Conservative Party members of his cabinet were opposed to imposing a huge new expenditure on the state, they nevertheless endorsed the promise of an appropriate postwar plan for universal health and unemployment insurance, housing, and free education. The Labour Party fully accepted the Beveridge report and, after its election victory in 1945, implemented the recommendations to set up the chief institutions of the welfare state in Britain: unemployment insurance, old-age pension, universal health care, and public housing. As Foucault shrewdly observes,

If I am not mistaken, this is the first time that entire nations waged war on the basis of a system of pacts which were not just international alliances between powers, but social pacts of a kind that promised—to those who were asked to go to war and get themselves killed—a certain type of economic and social organization which assured security (of employment, with regard to illness and other kinds of risk, and at the level of retirement): they were pacts of security at the moment of a demand for war.[32]

In short, the nation-state could no longer summon its moral authority over the people-nation to demand that citizens obey the call from their government to go to war and face death. Indeed, since the technology of warfare had changed, it was not only the lives of soldiers on the front line that were at risk. Even in their island country, British women and children were being pounded day and night by enemy bombers. Mobilized into trade unions and political parties, the people-nation had to be persuaded to enter into a social pact with the state. What were the terms of this pact?

Explaining the significance of the new institutions of the welfare state in 1949, the sociologist T. H. Marshall (1893–1981) outlined the story of the progressive expansion of citizenship since the nineteenth century. Beginning with the struggle for equal civil rights that could be enforced in the courts of law and progressing to equal political rights to elect representatives to Parliament and local councils, the process culminated in equal social rights to minimum economic security and welfare being provided by the social services and in sharing the heritage of civilized living through access to the education system.[33] I think we can understand the welfare state created in western European countries after the war as the most advanced iteration of Gramsci's integral state produced through the passive revolution of the bourgeoisie. Marshall's own analysis is significant. "There is," he says, "a kind of basic human equality" associated with the concept of citizenship "which is not inconsistent with the inequalities which distinguish the various economic levels in the society. In other words, the inequalities of the social class system may be acceptable provided the equality of citizenship is recognized." He adds, "Citizenship has itself become, in certain respects, the architect of legitimate social inequality."[34]

But even as he phrases the function of the new welfare state in terms of a progressive expansion of the universal rights that belong to all citizens, Marshall is careful to point out that this will not come in the way of the freedom of individuals to excel and flourish. This applies, in particular, to the system of public education that will become the key to the choice of occupations and social mobility: "The right of the citizen in this process of selection and mobility is the right to equality of opportunity. Its aim is to eliminate hereditary privilege. In essence it is the equal right to display and develop differences, or inequalities; the equal right to be recognized as unequal." And then, in a remarkable passage, Marshall describes how—through a process of successive phases of training, examination, classification and selection—students, beginning from a position of equal opportunity, would be weeded out in stages and deployed in different occupations and stations in life: "In the end the jumble of mixed seed originally put into the machine emerges in neatly labelled packets ready to be sown in the appropriate garden." Marshall was not apologetic for his choice of metaphor:

I have deliberately couched this description in the language of cynicism in order to bring out the point that, however genuine may be the desire of the educational authorities to offer enough variety to satisfy all individual needs, they must, in a mass service of this kind, proceed by repeated classification into groups, and this is followed at each stage by assimilation within each group and differentiation between groups. That is precisely the way in which social classes in a fluid society have always taken shape. . . . The conclusion of importance to my argument is that, through education in its relations with occupational structure, citizenship operates as an instrument of social stratification.[35]

Marshall's words are important since he was, in some ways, a major academic figure in the propagation of the ideology of British social democracy that would become hegemonic in the following two decades. Even as he presented the welfare state as the granting of universal social rights to all citizens, he nonetheless felt it necessary to point out, albeit in a mode of cynicism, that there was a certain inherent logic to a regime of power in which equal rights had to be tailored to satisfy society's need to produce useful individuals with appropriate skills and motivations. Thirty years after Marshall's lectures in Cambridge, Foucault would deliver his own set of lectures in Paris. Examining them side by side, we can see that Marshall's cynical account of the welfare state turns out to be a perfect description of biopolitical administration that proceeds simultaneously along two axes—one of disciplinary power that produces the individual, and the other of the regulation of populations in the mass. Enunciated in the language of universal rights of citizenship, the welfare state was actually the site of liberal governmentality.

The principal components of Foucault's analysis of modern power are well known. At the level of the individual, discipline involves training in order to attain a prescribed desirable norm: those who reach it are treated as normal, while those who do not are deemed abnormal, requiring special attention. Foucault calls this normation. But at the level of the security and well-being of a mass, there are two additional considerations: scarcity of resources that can be expended in pursuit of a policy, and uncertainty with regard to information and outcomes. There are several desirable norms that claim the attention of policy-makers. Hence, biopolitics at the level of the mass (i.e., governmentality) becomes an optimization problem. This, says Foucault, is normalization proper.[36]

The object of governmentality is not the people but populations. Populations have interests and proclivities that can be observed, identified, and played upon. As targets of the application of governmental technologies, populations are not to be confused with the ethical subject endowed with citizenship rights. Desired outcomes are to be achieved by tactics rather than by the force of law or, if necessary, by employing laws as tactics.[37] Viewed thus, liberal governmentality aims to optimize between the collective interests of populations, scarce resources, and uncertainty:

> It makes possible a self-limitation which infringes neither economic laws nor the principles of right, and which infringes neither the requirement of governmental generality nor the need for an omnipresence of government. An omnipresent government, a government which nothing escapes, a government which conforms to the rules of right, and a government which nevertheless respects the specificity of the economy, will be a government that manages civil society, the nation, society, the social.[38]

It is liberal governmentality that makes it possible for a machinery of social welfare founded on equal rights of citizenship to not only produce each individual as unequal in skill, ability, and fitness for productive activity but also to aggregate and reproduce those inequalities in the collective form of classes. Although Marshall was not aware of it, the seeds of the neoliberal critique of the welfare state were already visible in his optimistic portrayal of social democracy. Trade unions, for instance, had emerged to bargain collectively on wages, conditions of work, etc. But should they bargain with the government over their rights? "Rights are not a proper matter for bargaining," says Marshall. "To have to bargain for a living wage in a society which accepts the living wage as a social right is as absurd as to have to haggle for a vote in a society which accepts the vote as a political right." Yet just as governments were now intervening in industrial disputes, so also were trade unions intervening in the work of government. Marshall's suggestion was that this be regarded as a "joint discussion of policy"—a statement, we should not fail to notice, that confirms the operation of the integral state—but the unresolved tension between a mobilized and assertive trade union movement and the optimizing rationality of governmental technologies is palpable in his text.[39] Similarly, with the huge expansion of social and educational services and the recruitment of technical personnel to run them, it became incumbent on government to fix the relative incomes of different kinds of professionals. What should the salary of a doctor or a university professor be in relation to that of a schoolteacher or a factory worker? Marshall's answer is that "the claim is not merely for a basic living wage with such variations above that level as can be extracted by each grade from the conditions in the market at the moment. The claims of status are to a hierarchical wage structure, each level of which represents a social right and not merely a market value."[40] Was bargaining over such differential social rights, backed by the varying collective strengths of unionized professions, compatible with the equality of citizenship? Marshall was probably also unaware that the social inequality that would be produced through universal access to education—an inequality he believed was entirely legitimate—would, by the turn of the twenty-first century, become the single biggest social divider in Western capitalist democracies between a self-reproducing, highly educated, urban elite and a heterogeneous but discontented mass facing an uncertain future.

Without going into the specifics of the neoliberal critique of the welfare state, from its ideological statement in Friedrich von Hayek's *Road to Serfdom* to the technical elaborations of the economists of the Chicago school, beginning with Milton Friedman and Gary Becker, and many others since, it will be useful for us to indicate its main direction.[41] The first line of criticism concerns what was alleged to be the inherent waste, inefficiency, and corruption that result from a vast bureaucratic apparatus. The second line suggests alternative techniques for delivering support to groups that genuinely need it.

The first line leads to a set of policies designed to diminish the size of government and transfer social service sectors like health, education, retirement, old-age insurance, etc., to private agencies operating in the marketplace. The second line leads to governmental technologies of direct delivery of benefits, preferably in cash, to target individuals rather than providing state-financed social services to which everyone is entitled simply by virtue of the rights of citizenship. The charge is that subsidized universal services in areas such as health and university education are usually utilized most by the relatively affluent, who need them the least. Hence it is far better governmental policy to target genuinely needy individuals and give them cash support to buy such services from the market, which in general is a far better allocator of scarce resources than the artificially designed income and price structures imposed by government planners. Needs have to be identified and threshold levels fixed in such a way that they ensure that no one falls below a standard that is socially deemed to be an acceptable minimum. But the techniques of delivery must also ensure that the needy have the motivation to work and earn enough to no longer require government assistance.

Foucault notes some of the implications of neoliberal governmentality for the biopolitical management of mass populations. First, neoliberal governmentality avoids any attempt at a general redistribution of income. Relative poverty is not its concern; only absolute poverty must be targeted. Income inequality in itself is not a problem that government policy needs to address. Second, as Foucault notes, this will give rise to a new kind of stratification of populations:

> Full employment and voluntarist growth are renounced in favour of integration in a market economy. But this entails a fund of floating population, of a liminal, infra- or supraliminal population, in which the assurance mechanism will enable each to live in such a way that he can always be available for possible work, if market conditions require it. . . . They are merely guaranteed the possibility of minimal existence at a given level, and in this way the neo-liberal policy can be got to work.[42]

This is, of course, exactly the description offered by Marx of the "reserve army of labour" in industrial Britain in the nineteenth century.[43] As we will see in chapter 3, capitalism in the late twentieth and twenty-first centuries would produce a significant surplus population that would not be a floating labor force but instead simply redundant to the capitalist growth economy.

There is another—more directly political—aspect of neoliberal governmentality that relates to a concern we heard expressed by Marshall at the moment of the welfare state's birth. By directing social benefits at specific targeted population groups, neoliberal policies not only dissociate needs and interests from rights but also break up the ground for mass mobilization of benefit seekers. When health benefits, for instance, are disaggregated into separate policies, schemes, and agencies for, let us say, working mothers, retired men, infant girls, rural schoolchildren, etc., demands and complaints too become disaggregated. Since there is no general right around which a mass collective such as a national trade union can agitate or bargain, the field of social demands become thoroughly heterogeneous. This was the new political rationality that was aggressively, sometimes violently, put in place in Britain under Prime Minister Margaret Thatcher. The same rationality was disseminated in administrative technologies throughout the world in the 1980s and 1990s by international agencies such as the International Monetary Fund and the World Bank. As I will show in chapter 3, this change in governmental tactics would have enormous implications for democratic politics in our own time.

Contemporary political debates are often framed as contests between social democracy and neoliberalism, with the spectrum of parties and opinions being arrayed accordingly from left to right. I must insist, however, that a view that seeks, in a Gramscian spirit, to understand the history of the state in North America and western Europe as a continuing story of the passive revolution of capital will regard the two economic ideologies as two alternative sets of tactics in ensuring the hegemony of capitalist rule. Keynesian and neoliberal policies are by no means mutually exclusive, even though they are associated with two rival schools within the economics discipline, and even as the latter policies continue aggressively to undermine the former. Hence it is perfectly possible for ruling parties to decry big government and still run up unprecedented budget deficits or boost falling demand through a classic Keynesian method delicately disguised under the term *quantitative easing*, or for failing private companies and banks to be effectively nationalized by the infusion of state funds raised by tax revenues, only to be returned to their private owners once the health of the firms is restored. Also to be noted is the fact that, whether right-wing conservative or left-wing liberal, no Western government is able today to command its citizens to go to war and face death.

As we will see in chapter 3, an unpredictable mix of social democratic and neoliberal tactics, as well as right-wing and left-wing ideologies, is fundamental to present-day populist politics. What creates the opening for populist anger is the unresolved tension that runs through the universal expectation that governments should take care of populations: it is the tension caused by the contrary pulls of legitimate and illegitimate inequality. While the theoretical solution is offered by the formula of equality of opportunity, there is little agreement on whether a particular governmental benefit is a just reward for excellence or the affirmation of unjust privilege, a compensation for historical discrimination or the bestowing of new favors. The populist image of the entrenched elite exploiting a deprived mass of people is the result of this unresolved opposition that lies within liberal and neoliberal governmentality.

The twenty-first-century populist upsurge in the advanced capitalist economies occurs against the background of the tactical contraction of the integral state. Instead of the welfare state proclaiming its affirmation of the universal economic and social rights of all citizens, neoliberal governmentality brought in a new optimizing logic that operated in a field of populations endowed only with interests. It refused to acknowledge universal claims and instead selectively targeted groups and individuals to deliver benefits or impose penalties. Folding back the universal reach of the integral state meant a shrinking of its moral appeal to all citizens. Let us examine this process.

Interests and Rights

We have seen that under liberal governmentality, populations are distinguished from citizens, the former being characterized by interests and the latter by rights, even though the ideology of social democracy seeks to conflate the two. The distinction was made explicit and turned into a basic axiom for neoliberal governmentality. The individual, as a result, was split into a subject of interests and a subject of rights. The former was *Homo economicus*, the latter the citizen-subject.

Now, governmental policies of security and welfare are based on the premise that the interests of population groups can be known through observation. Groups could make their interests known to government by expressing their demands via statements, petitions, demonstrations, agitations, and such other conventional—and sometimes unconventional—practices of democratic politics. Governments could also take the initiative in collecting information about the interests of different population groups through surveys, investigation, registration, policing, and other methods of surveillance. As subjects of governmentality, therefore, individuals are endowed with interests and motivations that are, in principle, matters of governmental knowledge, most of which is public, but some may be subject to rules of state secrecy.

As citizen-subjects, however, individuals are characterized quite differently. Collectively they constitute the people who are the sovereign foundation of the state. The entire institutional structure of representation through which liberal constitutions function is based on the assumption that only the individual citizen can know his or her interests; no one else can claim that knowledge on the citizen's behalf. Hence citizenship must entail not only the right to vote in person in order to elect representatives to run the government but also the guarantee that each vote will have equal value since no one's knowledge could be presumed to be superior to that of anyone else. Further, the citizen must also have the right to vote in secret, confirming the premise that the citizen-subject is the best judge of his or her interests and is not obliged to reveal that knowledge to anyone.

There is thus a duality in contemporary liberal democracies between the subject of interests and the subject of rights, or *Homo economicus* motivated by rational interests and the citizen-subject as a constituent of popular sovereignty. But this duality raises questions: If individuals have interests, and could be constituted into population groups with interests, does it necessarily follow that in this role as subject of interests their knowledge is accurate? Is it not the case that people often have completely mistaken ideas of what their true interests are? If so, then would it not be right for a government that is committed to providing security and welfare to those it looks after to devise policies based not on what the populations want but what government, with the help of knowledgeable experts, deems to be in the best interest of those populations? The answer to these questions holds the key to several crucial issues I have raised earlier: hegemony and leadership, the balance of force and consent, and, most important, governmentality and popular sovereignty.

The question was raised as early as the aftermath of the French Revolution. The Jacobins, inheritors of the Enlightenment, believed they knew best what was in the true interest of the people and were therefore entitled to lead the nation-state on the people's behalf. True knowledge of society was thus coupled with the duty of an enlightened vanguard to educate the people into consciousness of their true interests and, in the interim, use the power of the state to serve them. Fichte's project of national education was also to be led by patriotic intellectuals with noble ambitions for whom mere civic love of the constitution was not enough. Of course, given the fact of the French occupation, the German intellectual elite did not have access at the time to the machinery of the state, but this lack, it could be argued, was more than made up for in the course of the later history of the German nation-state. By the middle of the nineteenth century, Marx would make his famous analysis of the two incarnations of Bonapartism—the first as the authoritarian, militarist, empire of Napoleon that accomplished the historical task of firmly establishing the legal and bureaucratic institutions of bourgeois society, and the second as a degenerate copy, pandering to the parochial sentiments of small peasant proprietors who did not have the class consciousness to represent themselves.[44] By the turn of the twentieth century, the authoritarian path to building a modern nation-state with an industrial economy, led by an organized party that rules on behalf of the people while coercively educating it into modern national subjects, became well established. The Kemalist state in Turkey was perhaps the prime example of coercive cultural education into modern nationhood, while the Soviet Union produced the most elaborate technical apparatus of central planning by experts to achieve rapid economic development.

The duality between the subject of interests and the subject of popular sovereignty, and the related question of enlightened leadership, appears in a 1929 play that retells the story of the French Revolution from the perspective of interwar Europe. Stanisława Przybyszewska, a young Polish communist, wrote *The Danton Case* as a vindication of Jacobin leadership in defending the true interests of working people based on the scientific knowledge of history and society. When the fiery young radical Saint-Just begins to speak passionately of the people, Robespierre interrupts:

ROBESPIERRE: The people—what does that mean,
Saint-Just?

SAINT-JUST: What sort of question is that? The people
means eighty-five percent of mankind, oppressed and
exploited for the barren aims of selfishness. They are
those who, because of poverty and work which is too
hard, cannot develop into human beings.

ROBEPIERRE: Yes. And now look at humanity in a lon-
gitudinal cross-section: it's a ladder of a thousand
steps, leading from big bankers to Negro slaves in San
Domingo. At every one of those steps, Antoine—there
stands an oppressor and exploiter of those below him,
who is himself oppressed and exploited by those above.
Separate then, if you please, the oppressor from the
oppressed.[45]

It is very unlikely that the historical Robespierre and Saint-
Just spoke of the people in terms of percentages and longitu-
dinal cross-sections, but Przybyszewska's language bears the
unmistakable stamp of the new twentieth-century discourse of
what was beginning to be called social science—knowledge
that would soon acquire universal disciplinary forms. The
scene also enacts the opposite pulls of popular sovereignty and
governmentality and the corresponding tasks of enlightened
leadership.

The Technical Administration of Things

Unlike the techniques followed by explicitly authoritarian
regimes, liberal or neoliberal governmentality proceeds by
accepting the preferences of individuals aggregated into population groups as social facts that reflect their perceived interests.

Much as Émile Durkheim defined them at the end of the nineteenth century, these social facts are structurally generated, expressing the beliefs, tendencies, and practices of groups taken collectively; they are things, not concepts, and must be observed and inductively verified as data.[46] With the rise of sophisticated statistical techniques in the twentieth century, these data would be cast in probabilistic rather than deterministic terms by distinguishing between individual events and tendencies that hold across large numbers.[47] Once known as things, social facts about populations and their proclivities could be tactically deployed in the administration of governmentality as forces acting on one another to produce a desired outcome. Indeed, probabilistic judgment could not only be deployed to randomize across a universal set but could also employ actuarial methods, involving appropriate and continuously updated algorithms, to distinguish between population groups with distinct traits and propensities—as, for instance, in the profiling of ethnic groups for the prediction and prevention of crime.[48] This, in fact, is what Asad describes so tellingly in his Ruth Benedict Lectures as the statistical language that has become the only medium through which the contemporary state can make moral appeals to the people.[49]

This realist view of interests and motivations, and the development of techniques for acquiring accurate knowledge about them, led to a proliferation of information about the so-called behavior of consumers, investors, voters, taxpayers, pensioners, and religionists—indeed, almost every conceivable population group with identifiable interests. Surveys and opinion polls, carried out periodically at regular intervals, would allow for comparisons, and the tracking over time, of the preferences of different groups. Indeed, once their status as social facts was accepted, it was no longer necessary, or even warranted, to insist on *Homo economicus* as a rational optimizing agent pursuing rational interests. The observed behavior of populations would show that they are subject to sentiments, proclivities, and passions that are often ill-informed, inconsistent, illogical, biased, and indeed thoroughly irrational.

This became a major theme of analysis and theorization in several disciplines of social knowledge. Advertising and marketing became replete with techniques to discover the tastes and spending propensities of different categories of consumers, to develop messages to appeal to those consumers' desires and prejudices, and thus to create demand for products. Indeed, advertising would emerge as the exemplary field that demonstrated how social knowledge could be skillfully used to shape the preferences of free individuals in a free society. Even in the domain of economics, the phenomenon of irrational behavior was noticed, if not seriously theorized, in the so-called herd mentality of stock traders. In time the findings of behavioral and experimental economics would lead to the claim—made most strikingly by Richard Thaler, the 2017 winner of the Nobel Prize in Economic Sciences—that the assumptions of rational optimizing behavior on which most of economic theory is grounded need to be substantially modified if it is to do a better job at prediction. In particular, Thaler says, economists must acknowledge that human behavior is characterized by inconsistencies and biases; hence the effort must be to discover how, based on the observed behavior of different groups of people, those biases might become predictable and thus susceptible to a judiciously chosen "nudge" delivered by the policymaker so as to elicit the desired behavior.[50] Similarly, experimental economics has emerged as a field that sets up—in the real world as opposed to the laboratory—purposively chosen small-scale sites with real populations and institutions in order to discover problems and test solutions in the implementation of governmental schemes.[51] The object in all of this is to gain greater predictive control over the uncertain behavior of populations and thus ground policy in a more realistic terrain.

The disciplinary study of irrationality in the political sphere is also old, going back to studies of crowd behavior and mass psychology. Needless to say, the twentieth-century history of fascism and a variety of authoritarian regimes that appear to rule with some degree of popular support have provided ample material for these studies. At the same time, with the emergence of independent nation-states in the hitherto colonial world, what were earlier the concerns of anthropology as the study of nonmodern peoples and their strange and irrational ways made their entry into the study of modern politics as problems of tribalism, ethnic conflict, religious identity, charismatic cults, etc.

Once understood as social facts, such apparently irrational behavior attached to particular population groups could be turned by the disciplinary social sciences into things that might be subjected to the play of forces generated by the law, the market, fiscal regulations, or administrative rules. Populations following their own irrational desires or prejudices could be made to engage, confront, avoid, emulate, or compete with others in such a way that the outcome desired by policy-makers was achieved. This is the technical administration of populations that the policy sciences strive to perfect. Thus, the careful study of ethnic enmities led to policy solutions such as the territorial partitioning of populations, the redrawing of boundaries for electoral constituencies, or changing urban zoning laws and transport routes in order to mix or separate, at particular times and places, different population groups in the interests of peace, security, control of crime, supply of labor, promotion of commerce, or any other desired outcome. Indeed, it is fair to say that at least from the 1970s onward, if not earlier, all social science disciplines have been mobilized for the task of contributing to the technical administration of populations as things.

The exercise of observing, analyzing, classifying, and deploying populations in a field of knowledge requires the distancing of the observer-expert from that field. Again, when recommending a policy, the expert is supposed to stand apart from the particular interests of a population group and propose a governmental action that furthers the general interest as defined after the many contradictory preferences have been optimized. The expert, in other words, operates in a field of discourse presumably uncontaminated by the partisan passions of social conflict. Curiously, this is achieved in most cases by replacing judgment based on experience and knowledge with numerical indicators of comparative performance—whether of individuals or groups or organizations—based on standardized data. The belief is that the public availability of such metrics ensures accountability, and attaching rewards and penalties to measured performance motivates individuals and organizations.[52] Thus, individuals within organizations, organizations in the competitive marketplace, and even governments vying with one another in a federal or global arena, will tout these comparative figures to boast about their own performance.

One consequence has been the emptying out of serious policy debate in the political arena. Real debates over policy now take place among experts, since they involve not political choices but questions of data, how that data are collected, the degree to which they are reliable, and how to interpret them. In other words, debates over political ideology have been set aside, for they are of no use in the technical administration of policy; instead experts debate over methodology within the various policy disciplines. This led directly to the result that, irrespective of labels, there was in most electoral democracies in the 1980s and 1990s a virtual convergence among parties in matters of socioeconomic policy. Continuous polling of changing opinions among the electorate led to experts fine-tuning campaign promises from every party directed at specific segments of voters in order to cobble together an electoral victory. As far as voters were concerned, there was little to choose among the various parties seeking their support. To further reduce the possibility of irrational political decisions upsetting the rational administration of things, several key areas of decision-making— for example, the control of atomic energy and weapons, the operation of monetary policy by the central bank, and the pricing of state-controlled energy supplies such as oil or electricity— were, by agreement among all parties, taken away from the hands of legislators and entrusted with independent regulating agencies composed of technical experts.

Are we now seeing a revolt of the people against being turned into populations as things? There is a curious section in Foucault's *Security, Territory, Population* in which he talks about the relation between the people and the population: "The people comprise those who conduct themselves in relation to the management of the population . . . as if they were not part of the population as a collective subject-object, as if they put themselves outside of it, and consequently the people are those who, refusing to be the population, disrupt the system."[53] This is, of course, a very different kind of distancing from that of the expert observer: Instead of stepping aside from the field of populations to study them from a distance, it is as if the people walk away from the roles created for them by the experts and refuse to act in the way policy-makers expect them to. Foucault was, of course, talking of an eighteenth-century French text in which the idea of the population as a well-managed and orderly productive force in an agrarian economy was being set out for the first time. But even though we have since passed through a long history of enshrining the people as the only legitimate foundation of sovereignty and identifying, classifying, knowing, and managing a plethora of population groups, the unresolved tension between the two collective subject-objects—the populations and the people—seems to be erupting once more.

This is the phenomenon we now call populism. However, as I hope to show in chapter 3, the matter is not quite so straightforward.

Where Are the People?

In 2013 a number of radical political thinkers were asked to answer a simple question: "What is a people?" Their responses— some brief, others extended—show how vacuous the idea of popular sovereignty has become under contemporary conditions of electoral democracy. Alain Badiou declared that in parliamentary democracies, the sovereignty of the people only means "the right of state. Through the political sham of the vote, the 'people,' composed of a collection of human atoms, confers the fiction of legitimacy on the elected." When attached to an adjective as in "the French people," it becomes a reactionary term. Only when a people is asserting its historical right to free existence that is being denied by an imperial power, or when a people excluded by the state from the sphere of legitimate recognition asserts itself, does the word acquire a positive sense.[54] Judith Butler argued that popular sovereignty is not exhausted by elections: "If parliamentary forms of power require popular sovereignty, they also surely fear it, for there is something about popular sovereignty that runs counter to, and exceeds, every parliamentary form that it institutes."[55] Pushing the argument further, Jacques Rancière proclaimed that

"the people" does not exist. What exist are diverse or even antagonistic figures of the people, figures constructed by privileging certain modes of assembling, certain distinctive traits, certain capacities or incapacities: an ethical people defined by the community of land or blood; a vigilant herding people by good pastureland; a democratic people putting to use the skills of those who have no particular skills; an ignorant people that the oligarchs keep at a distance; and so on.[56]

Yet lurking under the surface of these justified denunciations of the uses made of popular sovereignty by the rulers of contemporary nation-states there is a discernible longing for a people that, while not being original or authentic in the sense in which Fichte defined it two hundred years ago, is nonetheless virtuous, asserting an autonomous will and speaking truth to power. I am reminded of a scene from a play by Georg Büchner, written twenty-seven years after Fichte's addresses. *Danton's Death* is a complex, ambiguous portrayal of the founding moment of popular sovereignty. In this scene from the first act of the play, Robespierre is addressing a delegation of Jacobins that has come to Paris from Lyons to complain about the activities of forces opposed to the revolution:

ROBESPIERRE: No accommodation, no truce with men whose only thought has been to plunder the people and whose hope was to carry out their extortions with impunity, men for whom the republic has been speculation and the revolution trade! ... Be cool, virtuous people. Be calm, patriots. Tell your brothers in Lyons: the sword of the law is not rusting in the hands to which you have entrusted it. We shall set the republic a great example.[57]

This was the moment when, in Gramsci's words, a party of energetic leaders, relying on the galvanized will of the people, pushed a reluctant bourgeoisie forward to take up its position of hegemony over the French nation-state. But the ethical state that was to represent the ideal balance between force and consent, civil society and state, would remain elusive.

Why is it that in the last few years, there has been a sudden burst of popular energy around leaders and movements asserting the moral claims of the people-nation? I will examine the phenomenon of populism in chapter 3.

3

"I Am the People"

Passive Revolution: The Tactically Extended State

Thus far I have attempted to show that the evolving forms of class power in Western democracies in the second half of the twentieth century, embracing the era of the welfare state, as well as the era of neoliberal pushback, can be understood in Gramscian terms as the continuing passive revolution of capital. This involves, as Antonio Gramsci explains, a distinct move away from the classic liberal constitutionalist position—the ethical state, in which state and civil society are autonomous and perfectly balanced—to the integral state, where the ruling group exercises hegemony over both state and civil society, thus creating numerous overlaps between the two without, however, collapsing the distinction. Hegemony involves wielding an educative function over civil society. I have suggested that this hegemonic function has been effectively performed on behalf of the owners of capital in Western democracies through the techniques of governmentality, involving disciplinary and biopolitical power over individuals as well as masses. The welfare states of Europe mobilized the consent of the governed by pledging to guarantee the universal right of all citizens to unemployment insurance, health care, affordable housing, and access to education. In the neoliberal phase, universal guarantees were withdrawn through a tactical contraction of the integral state, and consent was elicited with the promise of unhindered access to the market where human capital was suitably rewarded; the unfortunate ones who failed were given targeted benefits to ensure a minimum level of consumption.

As we know, Michel Foucault strongly resisted the idea of linking the plethora of governmental techniques of the modern regime of power to any centralized and coordinated hegemonic function associated with a fundamental class such as the bourgeoisie. I believe the analytical gain derived from this rigid methodological position is canceled out by the loss of a historical perspective that enables us to discern significant shifts in the locus and intensity of politically mobilized power over longer periods of time. Consequently, I am unwilling to give up the Gramscian idea of fundamental social classes engaged in battles over the passive revolution. The only qualification is that, unlike in Gramsci's time, there is in Western democracies today effectively only one fundamental class in action—the owners of capital—that has both the consciousness and the organization to sedulously pursue its class interest; all other fundamental classes are demobilized and scattered.

In the meantime, other developments were occurring elsewhere in the world where capital was transforming traditional societies passing through colonial rule and postcolonial state building. As I noted in chapter 1, most of these countries of Africa, Asia, and the Caribbean were led in the 1950s and 1960s by nationalist leaders and parties with varying organizational strengths and depth of popular support. In some cases, such as those of the South Asian countries of Ceylon, India, and Pakistan, the structures of the colonial state were resilient enough to provide a firm scaffolding for the nation-state seeking to extend its control over territories and populations that the colonial state had largely left untouched. In other cases, the colonial state was itself stretched quite thinly across the landscape, sufficient only for its extractive purposes; postcolonial regimes often found it hard to unify the people politically into a lasting constitutional consensus. Nevertheless, vibrant democracies did emerge, as in India, for instance. The passive revolution of capital there did not, however, for the most part follow the path of the integral state. Instead it opened up a completely new trail.

To take the Indian case as an example, the bourgeoisie had to share power in the first decades after the independence of the country with large landed proprietors, while the bureaucracy manned by members of the urban middle classes played the leading role in a project of planned industrial development pioneered by the public sector.[1] The ruling Indian National Congress party, still wearing the mantle of successful freedom fighters, was able to build sufficient consensus at different levels of the democratic polity and hold the balance between the contending rural and urban classes. Electoral support in rural areas was largely mobilized through locally powerful landlords or caste leaders, while the reach of governmental agencies did not extend very deeply into most of rural society. As Ranajit Guha famously put it, the Indian ruling classes, following the path shown by the British colonial power, exercised a "dominance without hegemony."[2]

From the 1970s onward, however, following a brief spell of emergency rule under Indira Gandhi, the political dominance of the Congress Party began to wilt. Various regional populist parties emerged, reflecting the rapid spread of a democratic consciousness among wider sections of the people, emboldening them to make claims on the government. This was accompanied by a more accelerated pace of dissolution of the traditional agrarian economy. The state began to retreat from planned industrial development, and the bourgeoisie assumed a more dominant position as a ruling class. By the early 2000s, India drew attention as a leading emerging economy with the annual growth rate reaching 9 or 10 percent. Accelerated primitive accumulation meant a rapid dislocation of workers from the agricultural sector to urban areas, where they crowded into the burgeoning informal sector. It is in the attempt to govern these masses of otherwise unregulated populations that an entirely new set of techniques of governmentality was invented.

I have, in some of my earlier work, attempted to analyze these techniques—which, I believe, are by no means unique to India but can be found in many postcolonial democracies.[3] In brief, these techniques are premised on a distinction between civil society inhabited by proper citizens possessing enforceable rights and what I have called political society, peopled by populations with specific characteristics and demands that may or may not be met depending on contingent political considerations. Typically, the habitation and livelihoods of most population groups in the informal sector involve some degree of violation of the laws of property, labor, taxation, or public hygiene. But governmental authorities do not necessarily punish or evict these groups. Instead, in order to govern them better, the violations are frequently condoned as exceptions—without, however, endangering the structures of property or taxation that apply to civil society proper. The decision to declare such exceptions is temporary, based on a political calculation that takes into account the organized pressure these groups in the informal sector can bring to bear on government, especially in the sphere of electoral politics.

To better understand the historical novelty of the trajectory of the modern state in postcolonial countries, it is necessary to give up the dogmatic notion that if all the functionally related institutional transformations of modernity do not appear simultaneously, this must represent an imperfect or failed case. As Sudipta Kaviraj has pointed out, the particular sequence in which these changes are understood to have occurred in the West need not be repeated elsewhere. In that case, a different sequence of changes could well produce a different modernity.[4] Thus, to take an example, we could schematically represent the stages that have produced Western democracies through a sequence, with commercial society leading to civic association, then to rational bureaucracy, then industrialization, then universal suffrage, and finally a welfare state. If colonial and postcolonial history produces a new sequence in which, say, rational bureaucracy and universal suffrage precede civic association and industrialization, then the resulting state might be democratic without being a replica of the democratic state in the West. The approach involves, we may add, a Gramscian appreciation of the lack of synchrony between the formation of the nation-state as distinct from the people-nation and of the role of contingency in the unfolding of historical events. Democracies in postcolonial countries need not be versions of the ethical state or even the integral state.

I must confess there was some conceit in my choosing to call this zone of exceptional administration political society and claim that this was what popular politics was like "in most of the world." I did very much have in mind Gramsci's scheme of the distinction between state and civil society, with political society consisting of parties and associations performing the hegemonic function of educating civil society. What I wish to emphasize is that in large parts of the world, where the granting of formal citizenship has preceded the inclusion of a majority of the population into the recognized civic status of membership of civil society, the political function operates more as a means for groups to claim that, because of their special disabilities or misfortunes, their cases be regarded as exceptions to the equal application of the law. Perhaps the most ingenious and robust arguments for exceptional protections of this kind were made by B. R. Ambedkar in the middle decades of the twentieth century.[5] Since then such claims have become the routine stuff of democratic politics in most postcolonial countries.

What is important to realize is that this zone of the temporary suspension of the law does not follow from a recognition of traditional customs or the lack of modernity of these population groups. In other words, the logic here is not that of holding in abeyance the laws of property or representation for the so-called tribal regions of India by the colonial state in order to protect their populations from the depredations of commercial capital or cultural oppression. On the contrary, the populations that are sought to be governed by political society are the products of primitive accumulation and capitalist growth. Their location is entirely within the modern market economy and modern political associations.

The Indian economist Kalyan Sanyal (1951–2012) made an important theoretical intervention with respect to this feature of postcolonial capitalism.[6] Unlike the revolutionary force described by Karl Marx and Friedrich Engels in *The Communist Manifesto*, contemporary capitalism, Sanyal argued, does not transform precapitalist institutions in its own image. On the contrary, it often preserves and sometimes creates forms of labor and production that do not belong to the domain of capital. Indeed, this is a feature of the primitive accumulation of capital that was always implicit in its European career but has been now made plainly visible in postcolonial capitalist development.

Sanyal's argument goes as follows. Primitive accumulation separates the primary producer, the peasant or artisan, from his or her means of production. The means of production—principally land—is brought within the circuit of capital, while the peasant or artisan becomes a wage laborer in capitalist production. After this transformation is complete, capital becomes self-subsistent and there is nothing left outside it. But what if all the dispossessed peasants and artisans cannot be absorbed within capitalist production? One is talking here not of the so-called reserve army of labor that is periodically employed when jobs are plentiful and laid off when production is curtailed. What if there is an absolute, not relative, surplus population thrown off the land or from their crafts who cannot be included within the circuits of reproduction of capital? That is the situation today under postcolonial capitalism.

I believe it can be argued that even in the nineteenth or early twentieth centuries primitive accumulation in Europe yielded an absolute surplus population that was, however, politically managed through emigration and deaths in wars and famines.[7] Between 1815 and 1920, sixty million Europeans migrated to the Americas. A million people died in the Seven Years' War in the middle of the eighteenth century, five million died in the Napoleonic Wars in the early nineteenth century, twenty million died in World War I, and fifty million died in Europe alone in World War II. Deaths by famine and epidemic were common in Europe in the nineteenth century, the most devastating being the Great Irish Famine of the 1840s, in which a million and a half perished. In an age before mass democracy, such catastrophic deaths due to war, famine, or disease were far less costly to the ruling powers than they would be today. Postcolonial capitalism must operate under very different political conditions.

Sanyal argued that to ensure the conditions of continued accumulation, capital in postcolonial countries—even as it creates a vast new sector outside capital—does not require this redundant surplus population and need have nothing to do with it. Yet the political conditions for securing the legitimacy of capitalist domination dictate otherwise. The state must step in to ensure the conditions of survival of this population. This is where the policy science of development economics emerged from the 1960s to devise the technical means for an appropriate transfer of government revenues to create and keep alive a new noncapitalist sector, operating under market conditions but following the logic not of accumulation but of subsistence. With suitable subsidies or cash transfers, and by condoning the many violations of laws and regulations that apply to the formal economy, millions of surplus people are enabled to work and survive in the informal sector. Thus an entirely new set of techniques have arisen in postcolonial countries to continue the passive revolution of capital by tactically extending the reach of the state to target population groups in order to ensure the conditions of legitimacy for the dominance of capital. The bourgeoisie, having successfully whittled away the moral authority of the erstwhile developmental state, now exercises hegemonic power over civil society inhabited by the urban middle classes. But it can only exercise dominance, not hegemony, over the rest of urban and rural society with the assistance of governmental programs aimed at ensuring the subsistence of the vast population outside the circuits of capitalist accumulation.

This distinction between the formal and informal sectors of the economy is an analytical one. In the real world there are some informal enterprises that make the transition to a formally registered company operating by the logic of capital accumulation rather than subsistence. On the other hand, workers thrown out of the formal sector because their companies downsized, moved away, or shut down could be forced to make a subsistence livelihood in the informal sector. Besides, corporate business too could employ workers from the informal economy at subsistence wages without giving them the rights of organized labor. But despite these overlaps, the usefulness of the analytical distinction is compelling.

I have described these techniques of the passive revolution as characteristic of postcolonial countries. Yet they are not entirely unknown even in contemporary Western democracies. The techniques of governing immigrant and refugee populations in the United States or western Europe—populations that sometimes span more than one generation and often lack legal status—are clearly reminiscent of the tactically extended state. Thus they are allowed various facilities of work, habitation, education, health, banking, etc., without being recognized as proper members of civil society or given the privileges of citizenship. They live, in other words, in a zone of exception. The making of claims by such populations and the forms of associations through which such claims are made are also not dissimilar to those of political society. These are populations excluded from the pedagogical care of the integral state and governed through techniques that resemble the tactical extension of the state to populations regarded as exceptional.

Populism: Differential Demands and Chains of Equivalence

Populism is obviously the flavor of the season. Now that it hovers as an apparition over liberal democracies in Europe and the United States, a great deal of scholarly attention is being showered on it. An older historical literature, dealing with the Russian Narodniks, the American People's Party and Huey Long, or the Gandhian mobilization of Indian peasants, has been overtaken by analysis of contemporary populist movements in Western liberal democracies. What is not sufficiently known among scholars in the West, however, is that there is a much richer and more complex history of populism to be found in democratic politics in other parts of the world than is available in the European or Latin American cases.

Let me first set out the main conceptual structure of my analysis of populist politics by connecting it with the themes of nation, people, sovereignty, governmentality, and hegemony we have already encountered in chapters 1 and 2. I will then argue that whereas the rise of populism in Europe and the United States reflects a crisis of the integral state, populism in a country like India occurs on the site of the tactically extended state. The similarities and contrasts between the two phenomena have an important bearing on our understanding of popular sovereignty today.

Ernesto Laclau (1935–2014) has proposed an analytical framework for understanding populism not as a distortion or pathology but as a distinct political reason operating in the field of democracy. A key argument that shapes Laclau's approach is that populism is not defined by any particular political or ideological content; rather, it structures in particular ways the representation of whatever political content it articulates. Democracy is characterized by the expression of numerous demands by various groups. The heterogeneity of these demands has increased considerably in the twenty-first century because of administrative policies, some of which are linked to neoliberal economic doctrines that are designed to break up large consolidations such as trade unions and mass political parties. Governmental policies now seek to target specific population groups with specific demands that distinguish them from other groups. Laclau calls this the strategy of responding to differential demands through the logic of difference.

But all democratic demands cannot be satisfied, and when large numbers of such demands remain unsatisfied, they may add up to a negative condition. Even though the various demands are qualitatively different, they may be rhetorically linked by chains of equivalence as the unsatisfied demands of the people. Thus an internal frontier is created by populist politics separating the people from those who deny them their demands. Society becomes divided between an oppressed people and the powerful elite. Populist movements and parties create chains of equivalence through rhetorical, visual, performative, and other modes of representation of grievances. An empty signifier called "the people" is filled by a wide array of grievances, all signifying equivalent, unfulfilled, popular demands denied by the powerful elite that constitutes the enemy of the people. Because the demands are so varied, the signifier tends to be vague, lacking in specific policy content. Laclau argues that this is not necessarily a weakness of populist politics but rather a condition of its political efficacy.[8]

What Laclau's analysis also suggests is that populism creates a condition in which there is a tension between the logics of difference and equivalence. Thus, when a populist opposition comes to power and rules for some time, such as the Peronists in Argentina or several liberation movements in Africa, it becomes institutionalized within administrative structures and the logic of difference tends to prevail over that of equivalence. This produces a sort of state populism in which the populist content becomes diluted and loses appeal. It is, however, possible that "the people" operates as a floating signifier rather than an empty one, such that the heterogeneous elements that have to be stitched together into chains of equivalence could change over time. The rhetorical operation of equivalence is, then, metonymic rather than a simple metaphorical claim of similarity, with the parts changing places within the whole through performative iterations.[9] As we will see from the Indian examples, the ability to construct "the people" as a floating signifier is a major political achievement of successful populist parties.

Following the spate of new populist movements in Europe and the United States there is, however, a new literature that describes populism as a degraded form of democracy characterized by antielitism, antipluralism, and exclusionary identity politics. Thus, Jan-Werner Müller argues, principally from the evidence of populist parties in various European countries, that populists in power seek to hijack the state machinery, engage in mass clientelism, and suppress civil society.[10] Pierre Rosanvallon, who has endorsed nonelectoral actions such as popular vigilance, denunciation, and mock trials as valuable enhancements of democracy, calls populism a pathology "in which the democratic project is totally swallowed up and taken over by counterdemocracy."[11] Nadia Urbinati criticizes those who prefer to avoid the messy path of democratic choice and rely instead on experts to arrive at correct outcomes, as well as those populists and plebiscitarians who regard popular opinion as a field to be conquered by skillful demagogues or comprehensive ideologies. Democracy, she says, is not about the truth but about procedures that allow all people the equal freedom to exchange opinions, including the freedom to make mistakes and change their views.[12] Steven Levitsky and Daniel Ziblatt, after pointing out that democratic breakdowns have been caused not by military coups but through the ballot box, identify the problem in the abandoning by political parties of the unwritten norms of mutual tolerance and partisan restraint and thereby a failure to prevent "extremist demagogues" from seizing the leadership.[13] All of these condemnations of populism seem to echo an old liberal lament: "Too much Rousseau, not enough Mill!"[14]

I believe the most meaningful way to understand populism is to see it as a crisis of bourgeois hegemony. To clarify the point, let me recapitulate the main propositions I have established earlier:

1. The normative ideal of representative democracy is the ethical state in which state and civil society are autonomous and perfectly balanced, demands are aggregated and voiced in the private domain of associations, and government functions with the consent of the governed. There is, however, no historical example that can be found in the real world of modern nation-states that matches this ideal.

2. The integral state of the passive revolution is where the ruling bourgeoisie exercises hegemony by using the powers of the state to carry out a guiding or disciplining function over civil society without collapsing the distinction between the two domains. The hegemonic function may be articulated in two forms of the integral state. In the first, the welfare state recognizes universal social rights of citizens, articulated by political parties and civil organizations with mass following and exercised through multifarious biopolitical techniques of governmentality. In the second, instead of universal social guarantees there is a tactical contraction of the integral state that now promises unhindered access to the market and a safety net of targeted benefits to those who genuinely need help to maintain a minimum level of subsistence.

3. The tactically extended state of the passive revolution is one in which the bourgeoisie exercises hegemony over the properly constituted civil society of the propertied middle classes but not over political society inhabited by populations who may have formal rights

of citizenship but do not adhere to the practices of disciplined civic behavior. To allow these populations to survive, government must selectively extend benefits, suspend normal legal regulations, and treat these populations as exceptional cases—without, however, jeopardizing the structure of law and property that prevails in civil society. The zones of exception are declared and revoked tactically, based on political and usually short-term calculations of expected costs and benefits.

I will argue that even as populism shares a common set of characteristics in accordance with Laclau's explication of its distinct political rationality, it has rather different historical origins and consequences in the context of the integral state as opposed to that of the tactically extended state.

Let me first provide an analytical account of a half century's continuous history of populism in India. I will then return to the more familiar theme of contemporary populism in Europe and the United States. But before I do that, I will need to revisit a Gramscian theme I introduced in chapter 2: that of the relation between the nation-state and the people-nation.

Federalism as a Condition for Populism

The conditions for populist politics in India at the level of the central government are quite different from those at the level of the states. This is because of the difference in the way the identity *people equals nation equals state* operates at the two levels. This identity can be broken up, as we have seen earlier, into its components—namely, the people-nation and the nation-state.

The discourse of the nation-state was formed in India by a nationalist history mostly produced by scholars writing in English. The high points in this history of the state are the great empires—the Maurya, the Gupta, the Delhi Sultanate, the Vijayanagara, and the Mughal—all of which endorsed the historical possibility of state formations claiming extensive sovereign jurisdiction over much of the subcontinent. This history culminates in the British Raj, whose institutions of law, bureaucracy, army, education, and economy were transferred to the independent nation-state. Even as these institutions have been nationalized since independence, the continuity with the colonial state structure has been maintained by the use of English as the authoritative language of law, the central bureaucracy, corporate business, science and technology, and higher education.

The people-nation, on the other hand, was discursively formed through a much more fragmented, disparate, and contentious field of history writing carried out in print from the late nineteenth century, mainly in the regional languages. These histories are about caste, sectarian and religious identities, local and regional histories of political conflict and domination, social reform, linguistic identity, etc. Recall the history of races Foucault was talking about as the disorderly discourse of conflict lying below the surface of sovereign peace proclaimed by the state. The fragmented Indian discourses of the people-nation were similar, produced at the same time as the colonial state was declaring the reign of sovereign peace over the subcontinent. One may call these fragmentary narratives an old social history, quite different from academic social history, in which the achievements, tragedies, and aspirations of particular groups or communities were narrated. Academic historians writing in English to establish the legitimacy of the colonial or nationalist state tended to dismiss the old social histories as insufficiently rigorous in their methods and unacceptably ideological in their motives. But as politics acquired a more democratic mass base from the 1920s onward, this regional stream of history writing acquired new political significance. The regional languages became the principal medium of mass political communication, as shown by the Indian National Congress's 1919–1920 decision to reorganize its provincial committees along linguistic boundaries. The political process by which something called "the people" was mobilized as a political subject in different parts of India also energized the production of these vernacular histories. It is there, not in the academic histories of professional historians, that the people-nation was imagined as a political community, in each region in its own way. The democratization of the people-nation into large, relatively homogeneous, imagined linguistic communities led to the restructuring of the federal formation in India with the linguistic reorganization of states after 1956.

Madhava Prasad has clarified the role of language in producing the people as the subject of democracy in India.[15] He makes the important point that language does not necessarily have to exist in a primordial, natural, ethnicized community formed by the mother tongue. On the contrary, it is possible for modern democratic communities to be created, with the help of technologies of print and communications media and institutions such as schools and the bureaucracy, as open communities of speakers of a language; anyone who learns to speak the language can be included. Recall the two alternative readings of Fichte's nation we encountered in chapter 1. The language communities that operate in India's federal democracy are not closed ethnic communities of speakers of an original living language but rather open communities of all who have learned to speak it. Prasad also argues that these open language communities have been produced in the field of Indian democracy not so much by print as by cinema and television, whose reach goes far beyond those who have received formal education in the language. I believe the significance of regional language communities in India's federal democratic polity must be understood from this perspective.

Given this difference in the location of the nation-state and the people-nation within the Indian federal structure, the conditions for invoking "the people" as a collective political subject have become quite different at the two levels of the central government and the states. I will now pursue this distinction.

Indira Gandhi's Populism

Indira Gandhi was brought into power in 1966 by a group of Congress Party leaders who were entrenched party bosses in various states. She consolidated her power after 1969 by splitting the party, reaching out directly for popular support through slogans aimed at the poor, and reducing the strongmen to a minority wing of the Congress. Her populist stance combined such apparently socialistic programs as the nationalization of banks and mines and the abolition of the compensation paid to former rulers of the princely states with an agrarian strategy of "green revolution" based on providing state support to large landowners. At the same time, she also launched schemes of poverty removal targeting specific groups, such as scheduled castes and tribes, minorities, workers, and women, to be delivered by bureaucratic functionaries as gifts from the benevolent leader, bypassing the powerful local elites who were described as oppressors who had so long denied those benefits from reaching the poor.

Indira Gandhi's populism produced a highly centralized structure of power focused on herself as the supreme leader and dependent largely on a politicized bureaucracy for its functioning, abolishing the erstwhile federal character of the Congress Party run through strong chief ministers in the states. The developmental strategy of the era of Jawaharlal Nehru, with large public undertakings in the capital goods and infrastructure sectors and private capitalists in the consumer goods sector, was repackaged through the employment of a new rhetoric of state socialism, with the central executive structures of government playing the leading role.

These tendencies took the extreme form of the state of emergency in 1975–1977, when, in the context of a growing opposition movement through which the Gandhian leader Jayaprakash Narayan was trying to bring together all opposition parties, an adverse court judgment raised the possibility of Indira Gandhi being removed from office. She suspended the normal functioning of electoral democracy and the rights of assembly and speech, put large numbers of opposition leaders and activists in prison, imposed censorship on the press, and announced a twenty-point program that included liquidation of rural indebtedness; abolition of bonded labor; socialization of urban land; and special benefits to agricultural workers, weavers, students, and "weaker sections." In actual fact, the emergency gave unbridled power to officials and Congress politicians, who used it in an arbitrary and frequently violent manner.[16] At this point India seemed to have fallen into the trajectory followed by authoritarian regimes in several Third World countries.

Indira Gandhi's populism of the 1970s set a few trends. First, it established a form of state populism in which power was centralized in a single leader, no alternative leadership was allowed to emerge within the ruling party, and benefit schemes were implemented through a politicized bureaucracy. Second, the personality of the leader was projected through the state and party media as a benevolent protector of the poor and the underprivileged. In this Indira Gandhi was often characterized by commentators as a Bonapartist leader, standing above partisan, factional, and regional interests.[17] Third, despite the apparently socialist-sounding rhetoric, actual policies did not necessarily conform to any specific economic ideology since large corporate houses, big landowning farmers, and the urban middle classes largely dependent on the state sector all had to be kept within the ruling-class coalition. Fourth, the fact that Indira Gandhi called for elections after a year and a half of emergency rule showed that populist politics requires a periodic validation by the electorate in order to retain its credibility as a legitimate modality of government.

Yet Indira Gandhi's populism also revealed a major difficulty in establishing an effective chain of equivalence to tie together the people at the national level. With the exception of 1971, when the Bangladesh Liberation War raised the specter of a national enemy in Pakistan backed by China and the United States, the idea of the people's enemy so crucial to populist reason could only be actualized as Indira Gandhi's enemies. But these tended to shift over time. In the beginning, her enemies were the old Congress bosses who were said to be conservative and resistant to the progressive policies she was trying to introduce to benefit the people. Then the enemies became Jayaprakash Narayan and the group of Gandhians, socialists, and Bharatiya Jana Sangh party leaders who were said to be conspiring to topple her by spreading disorder in the country. When Indira Gandhi returned to power in 1980, her main enemies were identified as Khalistani agitators engaged in armed insurrection and terrorism with backing from foreign sources. In Laclau's terms, the enemy of the people was a floating signifier that was required to take on different meanings over time. Thus the varying elements representing Indira Gandhi's enemies had to be related metonymically such that any one of them could stand as "the enemy." But it also reflected the lack of a stable positive identifier that could provide imaginative and emotional coherence to the unity of the people; the only such signifier was the person of the leader herself. While governmental policies aimed at satisfying the demands of target populations representing potential constituencies of electoral support have proliferated after Indira Gandhi, there has been no populist regime in power in New Delhi until the victory of the Bharatiya Janata Party (BJP) under Prime Minister Narendra Modi in 2014. I will come to that episode later.

I think there is an important analytical distinction to be drawn from a study of Indira Gandhi's populism that is particularly useful in understanding the working of subsequent populist regimes in various Indian states. It is the distinction between the governmental and the ideological dimensions of populism. The first refers to specific governmental policies aimed at distributing benefits to target population groups with a view to eliciting support for the regime. At the level of technique, there is pressure for such policies to conform to a certain administrative rationality of legality, budgetary feasibility, and bureaucratic accountability. As such, these policies fall within Laclau's definition of the logic of difference and may be analyzed in terms of the administrative rationality of liberal or neoliberal governmentality. But they could become part of populist politics if the regime is able to present these policies as benevolent acts for which the beneficiaries should feel obliged to continue their support. This is the feature of mass clientelism for which populism has often been criticized, because it allegedly tends to keep electoral support groups in a perpetual condition of dependence on the regime. On the other hand, the question arises of whether such clientelism also introduces a certain transactional quality to the vote so that the promise of benefits has to be continually enhanced in order to prevent supporters from being enticed by a rival populist party. In other words, the charge is that mass clientelism leads to an electoral system of competitive populism that undermines and ultimately destroys the administrative rationality of government.

The second dimension of populism is the ideological one. This refers to the set of representations that makes it possible for a populist party to effectively portray the disparate unfulfilled demands of a variety of groups as essentially the result of oppression at the hands of the same oppressor. Needless to say, this dimension of populism operates according to Laclau's logic of equivalence. These representations, rhetorically produced through speech, visuals, and performance, make palpable in cultural and emotional terms the internal frontier between the people and their enemy. Just as the unity of the people, oppressed collectively, must be experienced and felt, so must the evil ways of the enemy invoke indignation and the will to resist. The rhetorical representation of the people and their enemy could build on existing solidarities such as ethnic, linguistic, or religious identity. But new solidarities may also be invented, such as distinctions between the wealthy few and the exploited many, or domiciles and immigrants, or a party long entrenched in power and those excluded. This is the feature of populism that draws criticism from liberals who claim that it necessarily tends to majoritarianism and antipluralism. There is also the possibility, as in the case of Indira Gandhi, of trying to represent the unity of the people in the person of the leader. Several of these different modes of representation of the people will be found in the many examples of populist movements and regimes in different Indian states.

Two points may be reiterated. First, the governmental and ideological dimensions of populism do not necessarily indicate any specific content of policies or representations. As we will see, the Indian examples provide evidence of a wide variety of populist policies, as well as rhetorical invocations of the people.

Second, I think it can be shown that the governmental aspect of populism inaugurated under Indira Gandhi has been ramified and expanded in numerous ways at both the central and state levels. The ideological dimension of populism has operated far more effectively at the state level, however, mainly because of the greater coherence of the regional cultural formations, produced by their relative homogenization through the regional language in the era of print, radio, cinema, and television and the institutions of education, public entertainment, and organized religious life.

I will illustrate these possibilities of populist politics by focusing on the southern Indian state of Tamil Nadu, but many of these features can be found in other states as well.

Dravidian Populist Parties in Tamil Nadu

Electoral politics in Tamil Nadu has been dominated during the last forty years by two regional parties, the Dravida Munnetra Kazhagam (DMK) and the All India Annadurai Dravida Munnetra Kazhagam (AIADMK), both claiming allegiance to the so-called Dravidian movement that took place in the first half of the twentieth century. This political and cultural upsurge, then led by the Justice Party and the Self-Respect Movement, attempted to mobilize non-Brahmin castes against the social dominance of Brahmins.[18] The interesting question is how the negatively denominated category "non-Brahmin" was crafted to provide a persuasive and emotionally powerful content of collective identity for a people. M. S. S. Pandian has traced this genealogy. He shows how the Orientalist representation of Hinduism, marked by a countless variety of practices and held together by a core body of Brahminical doctrine, was used by non-Brahmin leaders such as E. V. Ramasamy, better known as

Periyar, to castigate Brahmin domination, the Hindu religion, the Aryan race, and the reverence for Sanskrit all at the same time. At the other pole, using the Western discourse of rationalism, Ramasamy characterized the suppressed people as non-Brahmin, rationalist, Dravidian, and Tamil. At each pole the four terms were transitive, with each substitutable by any of the other three, as well as metonymic, with the part standing for the whole.[19]

What is important to note in the context of the later phenomenon of electoral populism in Tamil Nadu is that Ramasamy's Self-Respect Movement had a strong pedagogical content. He mobilized the anticlerical rationalism of the European Enlightenment, expanding it to include twentieth-century atheists such as Bertrand Russell and Vladimir Lenin, to demonstratively condemn religion in general and Brahminical Hinduism in particular. Alongside his campaigns against the imposition of Hindi, in the 1950s and 1960s he organized conferences for the eradication of superstition at which people were urged to give up religious ritual and embrace atheism. The manner in which Ramasamy and his followers carried out their campaigns was highly provocative, including the public burning of Hindu religious texts, the desecration of idols of Hindu gods, and the sexually explicit, satirical caricature of Hindu myths. The rejection of the Brahminical religion went hand in hand with the cultivation of a certain plebeian, non-Brahmin, Tamil culture that paid no respect to middle-class decorum, the latter being identified with the imposed cultural dominance of Brahmins.

Once the DMK made a bid for winning elections, however, it gradually tempered the strident criticism of religion, and its breakaway rival AIADMK gave it up altogether. Moreover, the anti-Aryan, anti-Hindi, cultural politics of the DMK, which after independence took the political form of demanding the right of self-determination for the Tamil people and secession from the Indian Union, was abandoned in the early 1960s with the acceptance of electoral politics within the given constitutional framework. By calling itself the All India Annadurai Dravida Munnetra Kazhagam, M.G. Ramachandran's party formally declared its allegiance to the Indian nation-state. From the 1970s onward, the DMK and AIADMK also showed strategic flexibility in forming electoral alliances with national parties such as the Congress Party and the BJP and joined coalition governments at the center.

Using Prasad's argument, we find that it was more the emergence through the non-Brahmin movement of an open community of speakers of a standard Tamil language—drawing upon the dialects of the non-Brahmin intermediate castes and gaining nearly universal acceptance through print media and cinema, schools and colleges, and public oratory—that enabled the Dravidian parties to develop and maintain a certain internal pluralism that allowed them to accept a non-Tamil like M. G. Ramachandran (popularly known as MGR) or a Brahmin like Jayaram Jayalalithaa as their leader. The Dravidian political identity was now defined as belonging to the anti-Sanskritic traditions that were strongly prevalent among the intermediate and lower castes, more Tamil than English, and opposed to the political elites of North India that wished to impose Hindi as the national language. Finally, internal pluralism was also enabled by an array of formal and informal associations that mediated between the party leadership and its mass-support base. Thus, DMK and AIADMK supporters also actively participated in caste associations, farmers' associations, and independent trade unions. And, needless to say, MGR fan clubs functioned as a major parallel network to the AIADMK.[20]

But there were limits to internal pluralism. As far as the governmental dimension of populism is concerned, while the entitlement of non-Brahmins to incomes and jobs was accepted—and frequently promoted—by the DMK and AIADMK, they would not allow any significant change in the structure of agrarian property since that would affect the political power of the dominant agrarian non-Brahmin castes. Further, both parties came to accept the reality of the existing structure of capitalist dominance in India. Since they were greatly dependent on revenues generated from the business sector to pay for their populist governmental schemes, the parties acted to facilitate the operations of Indian and foreign corporate business houses and offered incentives to invest in Tamil Nadu. At the same time, both parties actively promoted small- and medium-scale Tamil business entrepreneurs, who were mostly from non-Brahmin intermediate castes. Seen from this angle, populism appears to have added a new, if somewhat risky and disruptive, set of tactics to the passive revolution of capital. This involves a more complicated question, however—one to which I will return later.

The governmental aspect of Dravidian populism consists of sustained benefits for large population groups, such as reserved positions in government service and higher education for "backward" castes under the DMK and free or subsidized food for the poor under the AIADMK. These policies have been called populist clientelism and, contrary to usual bureaucratic rationality, they are intended not to create permanent assets but instead to yield immediate electoral gains. Populist clientelism works not so much through bureaucratic channels as through social networks within the cultural influence of the DMK or the AIADMK. Thus, even though backward caste reservations were, in principle, available to all listed backward castes, belonging to the DMK network definitely improved the chances of someone getting a reserved job when DMK was in power. With the rise of MGR and Jayalalithaa as leaders of the AIADMK, there emerged a more paternalist or maternalist populism, in which a benevolent leader promised to provide sustenance for the weak, protect them from the rapacious elite, and give substantive and regular benefits in the form of subsidized food, clothes, health facilities, books for children, bicycles, television sets, housing loans, etc.[21]

To return to Laclau's analytical framework, one of the key questions raised by the history of the Dravidian parties in Tamil Nadu concerns the ability of a populist leadership to keep changing the content of the floating signifier called "the people" in order to accommodate changes in its electoral support base. This must be achieved in the course of the constant iteration of "the people" in political performance. The attempt is not always successful. Thus, the historical identification of the DMK with the dominant agrarian castes, now fully entrenched in positions of social and political power, has provoked denunciations of the party and its non-Brahmin heritage by Dalit activists belonging to the lowest, formerly untouchable, castes.[22] But the party appears to have been unsuccessful in resignifying the chain of equivalence in order to hold together a heterogeneous and changing support base. On the other hand, the promotion of a paternalist or maternalist populism focused on the person of a supreme leader, as with the AIADMK, appears to offer greater flexibility in selecting and changing the appropriate content of the floating signifier called "the people."

Let us now consider the topic of the populist leader in some detail.

The Leader

Once again, Madhava Prasad has provided a valuable insight into the formation of the populist political leader in contemporary Indian democracy. In his book *Cine-Politics*, Prasad offers an answer to the question, Why do only some film stars in some southern Indian states succeed in becoming mass political leaders?[23] Even though his answer is drawn from the history of Kannada, Tamil, and Telugu cinema, I believe it can be restated as a more general proposition about the successful populist leader in India today.

The crucial element in this analysis is Prasad's observation that with the end of the sovereignty of the king-emperor, the dethroning of the Indian princes, and the political demise of great patrician families with pretensions to local sovereignty, there has been a dearth of embodied sovereigns in India. The abstraction called popular sovereignty, of which the only concrete manifestation is the periodic act of voting, lacks the substantive, personified, quality of sovereign power that protects, nourishes, and delivers justice. This, argues Prasad, is what cinema stars like MGR in Tamil Nadu and N. T. Rama Rao (popularly known as NTR) in Andhra Pradesh were able to provide.

It is important to emphasize that Prasad is not suggesting that Indian voters somehow cherish in their hearts a nostalgic desire for traditional kingship. Moreover, he explicitly contests the claim that the rituals of devotion to the star politician frequently performed by followers indicate a transfer of the religious sentiment of *bhakti* (devotion) to the domain of the political. What happens is that followers create relatively closed communities whose identity is anchored to the star. The initiative here, at least nominally, is with the people, not the putative sovereign: "These kings are chosen and anointed by the people: kings of democracy!" (176). Consequently, star worship does not assume that the actor's body is inhabited by the spirit of some already existing divine entity: he or she is not an incarnation of a god or goddess. Rather, the spirit is produced as an essence abstracted from all of the star's particular appearances: "The actor's body is endowed with his own sublimated spirit returned back to it as a henceforth imperishable feature" (174–75). This essentialized spirit makes the star capable of exercising the power of a sovereign.

Prasad goes on to explain why such a notion of sovereignty is consistent with the experience of subaltern populations. Even though they know that they have the right to vote, and are aware that they can use it to affect the choice of their representative in government, they do not thereby experience a share in sovereign power. With film star political leaders, Prasad says,

> the spectator relates, not as one sovereign to another, but as one element in a collective whose identity depends upon the presence of the sovereign star at the apex. There could be no clearer evidence than is offered by these films for the fact that the majority of Indians do not occupy the substantive subject position of citizenship. Their subalternity takes the form of dependence on such exemplary entities for any chance of a share in collective sovereignty. . . . It is more akin to a virtual socio-political order within which subjects feel securely located.
>
> (182)

It is thus a virtual community, formed around a sovereign who has been chosen by the people, that has to be hierarchically ordered if sovereign power is to be effectively used to offer justice and protection. The chosen sovereign is an ordinary person endowed with the extraordinary powers of stardom that make him or her familiar and yet beyond reach.[24] The sovereignty deficit of constitutional democracy is thus sought to be filled by the sovereignty effect of the star as political leader.

This popular choice of a sovereign is not, however, analogous to the Hobbesian contract, since not everyone becomes a loyal subject of a universal sovereign authority; there is an internal border that divides a true people from its enemies. The popularly chosen sovereign is expected to wage war on behalf of the authentic people in order to protect and nourish it against the machinations of the enemy. Instead of producing a sovereign peace, the sovereignty effect of anointing a leader often gives rise to the call for a just war. This is an important dimension of contemporary populism that has introduced in several Indian states, as indeed in many countries of the world, an unprecedented level of hostility and violence in the arena of competitive electoral politics.

Viewed thus, the verbal and ritualized demonstrations of loyalty expressed by followers toward the populist leader (which in India are usually described, by analogy with the religious domain, as acts of "devotion") could be understood rather differently. *Bhakti* or devotion to a personal god or sovereign involves recognition of the lord's superiority, praise for his or her actions, and a desire to participate in his or her realm. When a sovereign is chosen, a personal bond of subordination and loyalty is established that must be announced, displayed, and recognized for the follower to participate in the sovereign's domain of power.[25] Hence, what might appear to the skeptical observer as exaggerated and obsequious acts of sycophancy are indeed acts of political participation in a hierarchical world of power.

Prasad offers several examples in his book of how the sovereignty effect worked in the cases of Jayalalithaa, MGR, and NTR. Thus, the emergence of MGR as a star in his own right meant that the enthusiastic support base of the DMK expanded far beyond the identifiable interests the party was prepared to represent in its governing policies. By splitting the party and forming the AIADMK, MGR became the monarch of the vast illiterate, semiliterate, and powerless masses that were unable to represent themselves. The AIADMK under MGR, explains

Prasad, "may have been the first political party in India which represented no interests, only aspirations."[26] MGR ruled like a sovereign monarch—arbitrarily and despotically, repressing his opponents and showering gifts on his supporters. His successor, Jayalalithaa, chosen after his death by his fans over his wife, Janaki, continued in the same mode of the populist sovereign. After his split from the DMK, MGR was no longer the bearer of a political message from the party; he was himself the message. This indicates an important feature of the populist leader: he or she is not the agent of a pedagogical mission of a party or movement to transform the beliefs and practices of the people but rather reflects, responds to, and indeed embodies those beliefs. The distance traveled from E. V. Ramasamy and his campaigns to eradicate superstition is obvious.

There is another feature of MGR's star persona to which Prasad points that is important in understanding the role of the populist leader. In one of his films, MGR appears in the dual role of a king and a peasant rebel. The film ends with monarch MGR proclaiming his acceptance of all the demands made by rebel MGR, renouncing his throne and declaring, "Monarchy will end with me." MGR, in other words, is the self-declared last monarch. In another film, he is a plantation owner living in enormous luxury who decides to share all the profits from his estate with his employees and servants.[27] The narrative, therefore, is not that of a successful peasant revolt overturning the structure of authority but rather of a utopian but hierarchical order in which the one who possesses the power to be sovereign wields that power to benefit the people.

There is a final point to be made in relation to the popular cinema as an index of populist politics. The importance of melodrama as the dominant narrative form of the Indian popular cinema is well recognized.[28] The simple world of melodrama, peopled by suffering heroes and heroines, scheming villains and well-meaning buffoons, is ideally suited to depict a utopian world in which virtue is protected and vice punished. This narrative formula has been successfully deployed by filmmakers to rhetorically unify the heterogeneous publics it sought to reach. It fitted perfectly with the romantic idea of the people as the perennial repository of the authentic nation, unsullied by the corrupt touch of colonialism. It took but a small step to turn this ubiquitous cinematic mode into a general feature of the performance of the people in public life. I believe melodrama has become the generic narrative form of popular democracy in India. Of course, the formal properties of the cinema, embedded within what may be called performance capitalism, are necessarily different from those of political performance in the field of electoral democracy. But before we can begin the interesting exercise of mapping one to the other, we must first concede that a major part of contemporary democracy consists in performing "the people."

With the deaths of Jayalalithaa and the DMK leader Muthuvel Karunanidhi, the possibility of Tamil politics continuing along the same path of competitive populism led by sovereign-like leaders has been put into question. Yet I could give many other examples of populist parties and leaders, past and present, in other Indian states where the sovereignty effect is unmistakable: beyond NTR (who was also a film star) in Andhra Pradesh, Mamata Banerjee in West Bengal and Mayawati in Uttar Pradesh immediately come to mind, as do the parties Aam Aadmi Party (AAP) in Delhi, Asom Gana Parishad in Assam, and Shiva Sena in Maharashtra. Without multiplying examples, let me summarize what I think are the general features of populism in India's electoral democracy.

Populism in the Indian States

First, governmental policies designed to benefit large sections of the electorate in order to attract their votes are now routinely pursued by virtually all governments in India and hence do not in themselves constitute a distinct marker of populism. To be meaningfully understood as populist, a regime must represent itself in such a way as to define a border between the people and its enemy. In this respect, the linguistic communities at the level of the state governments provide more favorable conditions for populist mobilization than those at the central government. Second, such populist consolidations are usually built around a core of upwardly mobile intermediate castes with the social authority to mobilize other disaffected groups in order to form electoral majorities. Third, populist regimes adopt suitable tactics designed to win the next election and do not have long-term strategies for cultural pedagogy or social transformation.

The populist leader projects an image of benevolent protector of the poor and underprivileged. As such, he or she embodies sovereign power with which to deliver, arbitrarily and without regard for legal and bureaucratic niceties, justice and welfare for the people. The populist leader is authoritarian in style, runs a centralized machinery of power in which no challenger is allowed to emerge, and is not averse to using force to repress the opposition. But the populist leader must periodically renew his or her mandate by defeating competing parties in a popular election; populist rule is not dictatorial, nor is it justified in the Indian states, in contrast with some Latin American countries, for instance, by presenting it as the democratic alternative to military dictatorship. Finally, the populist utopian community is hierarchically ordered: the leader, chosen by the people, can exercise sovereign power to benefit them. It is noteworthy that several of India's populist leaders, especially women such as Mamata Banerjee, Jayalalithaa, and Mayawati, have been assigned familial positions of authority (such as mother or elder sister) in relation to the people.

Populism and National Hegemony

Before I conclude my discussion of populism in the Indian states and what it might teach us about populism in general, I must consider the conditions and limits of populist leadership at the national level, because it raises an important question about the passive revolution of the bourgeoisie in an integral state as opposed to the tactically extended state. When Narendra Modi came to power in 2014, he received unstinted support and massive campaign funding from big business. His slogan Sab ka Saath, Sab ka Vikas (Together with All, Development for All) seemed to be premised on steering decisively away from the remaining traces of state planning and regulation, ushering in probusiness reform of the tax regime and labor laws, and promoting rapid economic growth. Part of this was a promise to corporate business interests and the upper middle class; the other part was to recognize the aspirations of the upwardly mobile and the younger generation, who yearned for access to the glittering world of consumption. It soon became clear, however, that neither global nor national economic conditions were favorable for rapid growth. Over the last five years, the agenda of economic reform has proceeded in fits and starts. What has expanded at far greater pace is the reach of a dense network of data gathering, commercial penetration, and state surveillance through mobile phone services, electronic bank transfers, and mandatory biometric identification of all inhabitants of the country. On the other hand, specific demands from large electoral groups have become vociferous. The Modi government was forced to resort, even if reluctantly, to time-tested methods of governmental populism to quell the anger of farmers and disaffected dominant caste groups—though so far with little success. Major electoral reverses in three northern Indian states in 2018 only increased the urgency of populist spending before the parliamentary elections of 2019.

Theoretically this has raised the question of a choice between two paths of the passive revolution. Ever since the end of the dominance of the Congress in the 1980s, no national political party has held power in New Delhi without the support of an amalgam of regional parties whose mode of rule is thoroughly bound up with the tactical extension of the state through negotiations with various mobilized groups in regional and local political society. Several of these regional parties are also organized around strong populist leaders. Corporate business houses are often courted by these regional leaders with offers of cheap land and tax benefits for setting up industries in their states, yet the mounting costs of populist expenditure for the exchequer at both the central and state levels, as well as the arbitrariness and uncertainty produced by populist agitations and their periodically negotiated political resolutions, have been matters of serious concern for the Indian bourgeoisie. Modi's avowal of a developmental agenda appeared to signal both the ability as well as a willingness to abandon the selective and often random tactical extensions into political society and instead push for a hegemonic bid akin to that of the integral state. This declaration was enthusiastically embraced by big business and the upper middle class at the time of Modi's election in 2014.

But the BJP also has an alternative ideological agenda of Hindutva. Unlike populism, this carries with it a distinct and assertively revisionist pedagogical mission. It is founded on the idea of an original Hindu civilization, not unlike Fichte's imagined Germany, with an unbroken tradition of cultural nationhood that has survived centuries of political subjugation, first under Muslim rulers and later under the British. It seeks to create a homogenized public culture of Hinduness, itself a combination of reformist ideas of caste equality and inclusiveness mixed with traditional practices involving temples, rituals, festivals, sects, and holy men. It is carried out most pervasively and assiduously in the Hindi language, whose effective sway as an open democratic community stretches all the way from Gujarat and Maharashtra in the west through all of northern India into Odisha, Bengal, and the rest of the northeast. The ideological agenda of Hindutva is unconnected with the governmental agenda and can proceed quite independently with its pedagogical mission through schools, universities, publishing projects, cinema, television, and social media.

Leaving aside governmental populism, which is a feature that is common to all electoral parties in India, I believe it is important to stress the significance of the quite different political possibilities contained in the Hindutva agenda on the one hand, and the electoral mobilization achieved by the regional populist parties on the other. The latter builds on the affective sentiments that bind "the people" of a regional language community and draws an internal border that sets it against other ethnic groups regarded as exploiters or hostile intruders, or it pits the region against a distant and unsympathetic central power. Each language community is in itself a people-nation and yet is part of a larger nation-state. But given the constraints of constitutional relations between the states and the center and the existing structure of class power in the national economy, none of the regional populist parties can achieve anything beyond tactical electoral victories. As we have seen, no regional populist movement, including those like Ramasamy's Dravidar Kazhagam, which began with an alternative hegemonic narrative, has succeeded in carrying out a sustained mission of social and cultural transformation to create the people-nation in its own image. Populism remains mired in tactical battles.

On the other hand, the project of Hindutva is a hegemonic struggle to achieve a convergence between the nation-state as inherited through the transfer of power from British rule and a people-nation that is unitary, homogeneous, and transcends the various regions within India. It is often not realized that this hegemonic project is by no means a new venture launched by the BJP but goes back to at least the early decades of the twentieth century. It is a project in which intellectuals writing in Bengali, Gujarati, Hindi, and Marathi and belonging to the mainstream Congress nationalist formation enthusiastically participated. The idea that the people-nation is as old as Indian civilization itself—going back to the Indus-Harappa cities and the Vedic peoples and possessing a huge treasure of sacred and secular literature, principally in Sanskrit—is part of the everyday consciousness of most educated persons in northern India. In this hegemonic construction, the upper-caste Hindu male speaking a northern Indian language *is* the normative, unmarked, Indian.[29] State, nation, and people are made to converge around this normative identity. Not surprisingly, every other identity must occupy a place at some distance from the norm; the gap is expected to be closed through a process of cultural pedagogy and the deviant assimilated into the unitary people-nation. The Muslim emerges as the most deviant of all, representing several centuries of political domination and the vivisection of the country at the moment of independence. The Muslim is thus a perennial reminder of the enemy at the border: Pakistan.

The other narrative that held sway in the period of Congress dominance, and which often goes by the name of Nehruvian secularism, was largely constructed in the aftermath of partition as an inclusive ideology that sought to protect the place of religious and ethnic minorities within the definition of citizenship.

This was, however, largely a state-centered discourse. It did not challenge the civilizational narrative of the unitary people-nation; all it did was stress the cultural diversity that had been supposedly unified by the sovereign nation-state. Moreover, being a statist discourse, it was carried out far more effectively by scholars, journalists, and artists in English than in the regional languages. With the weakening of the Congress Party at the center, the BJP ideology of Hindutva, building on the prevailing vernacular sense of the civilizational centrality of Hindu India, has been able to accelerate its project of merging the nation-state with the Hindu people-nation.

The BJP thrust has been successfully opposed by regional populist parties in several states. Yet this opposition is restricted to electoral tactics. There is no significant counternarrative yet that can establish the regional forces as credible claimants to power in the central structures of the nation-state. Such a counterhegemonic narrative, if it is to build upon the populist mobilizations in the regions, must project the idea of the Indian nation-state as one founded not by a unitary people-nation but by a number of federating peoples who came together to form a sovereign state. A federated "peoples-nation" would allow for not only the equal presence within it of many languages, religions, and ethnicities but also of several civilizational narratives, including those of the minority religions, the Dravidian languages, the Dalit castes, and the tribal peoples of central and northeastern India.[30] The regional populist movements have been unable to formulate a transformative hegemonic strategy of this kind.

Since 2014, with the BJP at the center of government, the ideological pursuit of Hindutva has been carried out, with varying degrees of enthusiasm and persistence, in different parts of the country. On the one hand, this has involved tenacious work by dedicated Hindutva volunteers in local initiatives to provide educational services, health care, and other social services, especially to lower-caste and tribal communities in order to enable them to claim a respectable place within the Hindu fold.[31] On the other hand, there has also been a significant rise in murderous attacks on individual Muslims and those allegedly holding "antinational" or "anti-Hindu" views, carried out by vigilante groups that seem to operate with impunity in BJP-ruled states. One part of this campaign seeks to educate and include while the other terrorizes and excludes.

And yet, as the BJP prepares for reelection in 2019, its campaign is centered almost entirely on the personality of Narendra Modi. All the resources of publicity have been mobilized to cultivate the image of a strong leader who can share the world stage with the great powers, protect the country against its enemies, fight foreign-sponsored terrorism, and promote economic growth that will benefit all. In a tactic reminiscent of Indira Gandhi's populism, the nation's external enemy—Pakistan—is metonymically connected to the opposition parties and leaders in order to constitute the floating signifier called "the enemy of the people": those who oppose Modi are the nation's enemies, and hence the people's enemies. The early promise of a hegemonic push toward an integral state seems to have been given up—at least for now. What is under way is an electoral battle between Modi's populist leadership and a tactical combination of several regional populisms. The bourgeoisie, it appears, has to settle for dominance, not hegemony, and accept the inevitability of populist uncertainty and excess.

Keeping in mind our earlier discussions on hegemony and the multiple forms of the passive revolution, I have emphasized the distinction between the transformative cultural project of Hindutva and the electoral competition between the BJP and its opponents because of their different political implications. There is little doubt that, irrespective of election results, the pedagogy of Hindutva will continue to claim that a strong and unified nation-state must rest on the support of a unitary and homogeneous people-nation. As long as there is no alternative narrative that can bind the regional popular mobilizations into a credible historical bloc at the level of the center, the BJP can only be challenged through tactical electoral alliances. Politics will remain confined to competitive populism seeking to assuage the demands of various sections of political society

The Sovereign People and Their Representatives

The key to the technique of making provisionally negotiated concessions to population groups in political society is the formulation of an exception to the normal rule. Thus, specific target groups of poor or underprivileged persons may be given government benefits that are not available to others, or hawkers and slum squatters may be allowed to continue their illegal occupation of public space on the ground that such exceptional measures are necessary to provide them with the minimum conditions of decent livelihood. But the exceptions must not endanger the normative structure of law and property that applies to properly constituted civil society. Hence the justifications, whether informed by humanitarian sentiment or pragmatic politics, have to be phrased in appropriate legal-administrative language so as not to violate existing laws and run afoul of the courts.

But when heterogeneous demands from political society are successfully strung together into a populist claim, it is no longer advanced in the restrained language of the exception but voiced as a righteous demand of the popular majority. Regardless of its consistency with existing laws, the claim is said to be justified because it is the people's will as expressed by their vote.

Since the sovereign people have spoken, its voice must prevail over all other considerations such as convention, precedent, rule, or norm.

We have seen this claim appear in Indian populism as a feature of what I have called the tactically extended state. But it is equally apparent in contemporary populism in the West. Indeed, implicated in this feature of populism is a latent and never quite explicitly resolved problem of the modern state— namely, the relation between popular sovereignty and representative government.

In a carefully researched study, Richard Tuck has reminded us that ever since Jean Bodin in the sixteenth century, there has persisted in all thinking about modern democracy in the West a distinction between sovereignty and government.[32] The former, said Bodin, was the power to make laws and to appoint and dismiss the officers of government, and the latter the power to occupy and administer the offices. Thus it was possible for Roman dictators to have absolute and untrammeled powers of government without having sovereignty, since they were elected by the people. As the idea of democratic government rose to prominence in the seventeenth century, the distinction was used—for example, by Hugo Grotius—to explain how the Romans remained the same people even when they were ruled at various times by kings, consuls, and emperors; not just that, a people could retain its sovereignty even when it was ruled by a foreign civitas. But Grotius also introduced another distinction that, according to Tuck, was to have a lasting impact on democratic thought. The sovereign people as a whole, Grotius said, was only a common subject of sovereignty: it was, as it were, the community bound by a single constitution within which the laws had force. But it was by no means the proper subject of sovereignty since, except for rare revolutionary moments, the people as a whole neither made laws nor had jurisdiction over administration. The people, in other words, were sovereign without exercising sovereign power.

The revolutionary era inaugurated by events in the Americas and France, even as it enshrined popular sovereignty at the very core of the modern state, did not confuse sovereignty with government. Jean-Jacques Rousseau argued passionately that the general will could be neither divided nor alienated, and that the popular legislative assembly had to meet at scheduled intervals to exercise its sovereign power, but that did not mean that the people could not elect representatives to carry on the business of government. It only meant that the elected deputies could not represent a people in its role as sovereign. During the tumult of the French Revolution, the exact location and role of popular sovereignty was very much at issue. Tuck argues that even though they were thoroughly defeated at the time, it was the Girondins whose views have had the most lasting effect on modern democracy: they had insisted that once the constituent power of the sovereign people was exercised through a plebiscite, the ordinary business of lawmaking and government should be left to elected deputies. The distinction between sovereignty and government underlying the Girondin position has been worked upon in subsequent history to turn the people into a sleeping sovereign. An Alabama legislator once put the matter quite plainly during a debate on secession in the days leading up to the American Civil War: "Ours is not a pure Democracy—that is a government by the people—though it is a government of the people. Ours is a representative government, and whatever is done by the representative in accordance with the Constitution is law; and whatever is done by the deputy in organizing government is the people's will."[33] Two years later, as the tide of the Civil War turned in favor of the Union, Abraham Lincoln, speaking at Gettysburg, cloaked this unvarnished description with what would become the most oft-repeated cliché about democracy. We now know, however, that democracy as actually practiced is formally a government *of* the people; most volubly and demonstrably, it is a government *for* the people; but nowhere is it a government *by* the people.

There are sophisticated arguments that have been advanced by the modern social sciences to fortify this understanding of democracy. An important line of argument concerns the manner in which a people might express its will. It is well understood that unanimity would be an impossible condition to meet in any large popular assembly. From the time of the French Revolution, political experts (the Marquis de Condorcet, for instance) have been concerned with devising fair and rational voting procedures through which assemblies arrive at collective decisions. In the years after World War II, particularly in the context of the widely expanded welfare policies of democratic governments, an entire field of social choice theory developed to tackle the problem of collective decision-making. Following Kenneth Arrow's landmark 1951 demonstration that it is impossible to convert the ranked preferences of voters between more than three alternatives into ranked choices of the entire collective while meeting certain logical and nonarbitrary rules, numerous theorists have devised voting methods—all of which, however, require a certain degree of arbitrary specification. It is well understood now that every democratic voting procedure is dependent on a set of arbitrary rules that, if altered, could produce a very different collective result.

The implication of these findings of social choice theory for our understanding of democracy was summed up in 1982 by William Riker, a founder of rational choice political theory (and, incidentally, my doctoral dissertation adviser at the University of Rochester). His argument was as follows. Voting outcomes depend on decision rules of which there may be many, each with strong justification. Each such rule may yield a different outcome. Thus, if I were to give a very familiar example, the outcome of the U.S. presidential election of 2016 would have been quite different had it been decided by a national popular vote rather than by the arbitrarily constituted electoral college. Since the outcome of a vote is dependent on the particular decision rule that has been adopted, Riker argued that there could be no ground for declaring that result as the people's will, since it is merely a decision without any moral weight. Additionally, since people vote with the knowledge that they are voting under a particular decision rule, there is no way of knowing if an actual decision would have been different under a different decision rule. Again, as we all know, a voter's choice may be manipulated by tactical voting (i.e., voting not for one's first choice but for a likely winner in order to prevent a less preferred candidate from winning) or by controlling the agenda on which one votes. Yet there is no way by which it can be determined if the actual outcome has been affected by manipulation. Hence, Riker claimed, there is no moral sanctity to electoral decisions. Populist claims that an election result, being the people's will, is a morally binding mandate cannot be sustained; indeed, there is no possible procedure by which the people can know for certain what its collective will is. Consequently, such a populist claim is nothing but a license for coercion.[34]

Riker was defending a view of democracy—he called it liberal in the Madisonian sense—that holds that the function of voting is simply to make officials accountable, and no more. To achieve this it is necessary that voting be popular and sufficient that elected officials have limited tenure. Nothing further can be claimed on behalf of the popular vote. According to this liberal view of democracy, the people are, and ought to be, merely the sleeping sovereign.

The difficulty is that laws made by elected representatives are binding for all. The consequences of many such legislative acts are irreversible; changing the representatives at the next election does not necessarily rectify the damage caused by a bad law. Sometimes, as under the constitutional rules of the United States, an elected legislature in league with the chief executive could change the character of the highest judicial body for the next two or three decades. Additionally, an elected body is often empowered to alter the voting procedures or the demarcation of electoral constituencies for the election of subsequent legislators. Contrary to Riker's claim on behalf of a limited view of liberal government, the consequences of manipulation and controlling the agenda go far beyond the problem of determining the robustness of decision rules.

For one, there is the question of the power wielded by the numerically tiny group of wealthy and propertied people who make massive campaign contributions and thereby control the agenda. Next, the emergence of weekly opinion polls and the dissemination of varied political messages from the same leader or party, fine-tuned for select target groups of voters through the visual and electronic media, make it nearly impossible to define what a representative actually stands for. At the same time, given the virtual omnipresence of digital recording technologies and methods of retrieval of archived footage, the evidence of elected representatives saying different things at different times to different people, and then doing something that is inconsistent with all of those promises, is there for everyone to see. The result is widespread distrust of elected representatives. It is by no means an exaggeration to say that at the turn of the twenty-first century, Western liberal democracies faced a deep crisis of representation. If we recall that the hegemonic function in advanced capitalist societies is led and guided precisely by the institutions of representation run by political parties, leaders, and ideologues, we will see that the crisis of representation is in fact a crisis of the integral state.

Contemporary populism in the United States and western Europe is a response to this crisis of the integral state. The most palpable symptom of the crisis is the collapse, in one country after another, of the credibility of traditional political parties and leaders whose organizational resources and moral legitimacy served as the pillars on which bourgeois hegemony had rested for at least the last half a century, if not longer. Those representatives—the hitherto benign and often revered public faces of class power—are now being targeted by populist campaigners as a political class that has sold out to the moneybags and entrenched itself in every institution of power. Politicians are reviled for swaying from one position to another and not having a mind of their own, for surrendering the power of decision-making to opaque and often nameless bodies of technocrats who operate behind a thick veil of recondite expertise and are not accountable to the people. Together the politicians and the experts make up the entrenched elite that has become the enemy of the people.

This internal border separating the true people from their enemies is not naturally, or even historically, given; it has to be created rhetorically and imaginatively. That, as Laclau pointed out, is what populist movements and leaders try to do. What can we say about this process from our survey of fifty years of Indian populism?

First, the internal border tends to fall along some recognizable fault line of cultural identity. The Tamil case shows the remarkable feat of the leaders of the Dravidian movement in imbuing the negative identity of "non-Brahmin" with a positive content powerful enough to distinguish itself from the Aryan, Sanskritic, Brahmin enemy. The test of a populist movement is, however, its ability to adjust and even transform the specific cultural content of the floating signifier called "the people" to suit changing electoral or strategic conditions. This is not easy.

Second, the most effective way in which the floating signifier can be made to work in a changing electoral field is to tie
the identity of "the people" to the person of a leader. By choosing and anointing a leader with the attributes of sovereignty, the
people—the devoted followers—participate in his or her sovereign realm. The leader is expected to be authoritarian, wield
arbitrary powers in ways he or she knows best, wage war on the
enemy, cut through the maze of procedure and convention that
only protects the powerful oligarchs, and deliver justice for the
people.

Third, the immediate measure of success of a populist regime
or leader is scoring wins against the enemy. As the Indian example shows, populism is not conducive to a long-term pedagogical project of educating a people into better citizenship. On the
contrary, the leader must embody the values and ways of life of
ordinary people, reveal an authentic personality, speak plainly
and fearlessly, and reject the cultural pretensions of the elite.

Fourth, the prominence of film celebrities among Indian
populist leaders is an index of the power of visual communications, such as cinema, television, and social media, in contemporary democratic mobilization. Populist leaders communicate most effectively when they become familiar everyday faces
that people believe they know intimately enough to pledge personal faith in them or, by contrast, reject their advances as inau-
thentic and untrustworthy. Populism also thrives on melodramatic narratives in which honesty triumphs over cynicism, good
over evil. The cinematic idiom has a far more generic presence
in contemporary democracy everywhere than is conceded in
political theory.

What countries like India have witnessed for several decades
has now arrived on the placid shores of Western liberal democracies. When liberal commentators feel bewildered by

Donald Trump's outlandish leadership style, they would do well to remember that popular sovereignty is no longer easily tamed by protocols of constitutional patriotism or persuaded by long tracts of philosophical prose debated in coffeehouses. Nor can the sudden import of practices regarded as typical of the Third World be explained by resort to concepts such as tribalism, which is redolent of colonial anthropology. Populism in countries like India is not a remnant of premodern clan warfare but a product of the most modern phase of democratic politics in which millions of powerless and aggrieved people have formal rights of citizenship. When populist leaders in the West today behave like absolute monarchs, use official positions to enrich themselves and their families, distribute favors to their cronies, bend agencies of law enforcement and regulation to partisan or personal ends, or make outrageously grand claims about their achievements, one ought to think about the sovereignty effect produced by the aspirations of subaltern populations who respond to their sovereignty deficit by choosing a sovereign of their own.

Cynicism and Utopia

Let me conclude by returning to the founding moment of popular sovereignty. The story of Georges Danton and Maximilien Robespierre was retold in the 1983 film *Danton* by the Polish film director Andrzej Wajda. In the scene where Danton is charged at the National Convention of plotting against the republic, Wajda has Danton shout, "I will go on speaking to the end, because I am immortal. For I am the people, the people are with me. You murderers will be judged by the people." We know, of course, that the people did not save Danton, a well-liked and approachable man of the people, from the guillotine; nor did Robespierre, the reclusive paragon of revolutionary virtue, escape the same fate. Since then, for more than two centuries, the utopia of popular sovereignty has been a favorite object of the cynical manipulation of power. I will end by making a final remark on current attempts to rouse the sleeping sovereign.

Many contemporary commentators want to distinguish between left-wing and right-wing, or progressive and reactionary, populism. These distinctions themselves indicate that populism itself need have no specific ideological leanings in terms of the traditional left-right division. But sympathetic observers often point to Hugo Chávez, Luiz Inácio Lula da Silva, or Evo Morales in Latin America and contrast them with Rodrigo Duterte in the Philippines, Recep Tayyip Erdoğan in Turkey, or Victor Orbán in Hungary to suggest that left-wing populist regimes could bring about significant improvements in the conditions for a dignified life for poor and marginal populations. Yet every such positive assessment has to be qualified by the recognition that these improvements were secured at the cost of violent repression, the muzzling of the opposition, unbridled corruption, the weakening of public institutions, and the ultimate jeopardy of those very achievements. Instead of a strategic vision of social transformation, these supposedly left-wing regimes, by the innate logic of populist rationality, are more eager to exploit tactical opportunities for expanding and prolonging their tenure in power. Winning the next election is more important than creating or securing institutions to preserve the gains of progressive reform. That is why many enthusiastic followers of populist parties such as the Aam Aadmi Party in India, Podemos in Spain, or Syriza in Greece had to face bitter disappointment when promises of radical change were jettisoned for the sake of short-term electoral success. That is also why the supposedly left-wing Movimento 5 Stelle has found it acceptable to join the thoroughly right-wing Lega in forming a government in Italy.

We go back once again to the passive revolution. Just as organized forces on the left, for tactical reasons, often hitch their fortunes to the bandwagon of a populist party, so could the owners of capital choose to find a way out of the crisis of the integral state by betting on a populist leader. Populism has emerged as one more tactical resource in the continuing passive revolution of capital. Sure enough, it is a risky tactic; if a populist Syriza party has been effectively used by the big European banks to impose economic austerity on a restive Greek population, the resort to the popular referendum has ended up in a disastrous mess in Britain. And even though Donald Trump has delivered significant tax breaks to the wealthy, the jury is still out on whether his war on global institutions of trade will offer American capitalists some new resources to fight the challenge posed by China. But, as Gramsci was so keenly aware, the passive revolution is a terrain of warfare in which contingency, opportunism, accident, and strength of will often win the day.

As far as the people themselves are concerned, their hopes were well expressed a hundred years ago by the American poet Carl Sandburg:

I am the people—the mob—the crowd—the mass.
... The Napoleons come from me and the Lincolns.
They die. And then I send forth more Napoleons and Lincolns.
... Sometimes I growl, shake myself and spatter a few red drops for history to remember. Then—I forget.
When I, the People, learn to remember, when I, the people, use the lessons of yesterday and no longer

forget who robbed me last year, who played me for a
fool—then there will be no speaker in all the world say
the name: "The People," with any fleck of a sneer in
his voice or any far-off smile of derision.
The mob—the crowd—the mass—will arrive then.[35]

A hundred years later, the people have still not arrived.

Afterword: The Optimism of the Intellect

These Ruth Benedict Lectures were delivered at Columbia University in April 2018. When I finished, several audience members came up and complained that these were the most pessimistic words they had ever heard me speak. Had I given up the hope I had always placed in the creative energies of the people? I must confess I was taken aback by the question. I think I owe an answer to the readers of these published lectures. Here I will I discuss in turn what I see as the possibilities and dangers surrounding popular political initiatives in Western and postcolonial countries today.

Crisis

Two European countries, both of them imperial powers until the mid-twentieth century and both celebrated in the history of modern democracy, have figured prominently in my discussion on how the idea of popular sovereignty has been used to produce bourgeois hegemony in its different forms. It would be instructive to compare the ways in which that hegemony has been brought to a crisis in the two countries. In one the crisis is manifested in the failure of elected representatives belonging to the major political parties to carry out an explicit decision made by the people in a referendum called for by the government. In the other, weekend demonstrations by thousands of leaderless people in cities and towns across the country have lasted for several months and show no signs of abating, despite repeated concessions from the government. The crisis appears in the former case as an unresolvable impasse at the top echelons of power, while in the latter it points to a smoldering substratum of pent-up anger that refuses to die.

A popular referendum was proposed in 2015 by the Conservative Party prime minister David Cameron as a bargaining ploy to extract from the European Union (EU) a concession that would allow the United Kingdom to retain control over immigration and refuse further integration with Europe. He did not get his way. Pushed by Euroskeptics in his party and the virulently anti-immigration UK Independence Party, Cameron made an election pledge to put the question of Britain's continued membership in the EU to a popular vote. In June 2016, when asked to make a simple choice between remaining in the EU or leaving it, 52 percent of British voters picked the latter option. The result, known as Brexit, was utterly unexpected and opened up major rifts within both of Britain's main political parties. Cameron resigned, and Theresa May was chosen to lead the country in negotiations with the EU on the terms of an immensely complicated separation. Once the legal procedures of formalizing the decision were concluded in March 2017, it was announced that the United Kingdom would leave the EU two years later, giving sufficient time to officials on both sides to sort out the massive technical details. Hoping to strengthen her hand in Parliament, May called for a snap election. It was a bad miscalculation, because the Conservatives lost their majority and had to cobble a coalition with a party from Northern Ireland, complicating even further the problems of separation along the Irish border.

The scheduled date of March 29, 2019, came and went, but May was unable, despite three attempts, to get the withdrawal plan she had negotiated with the EU approved by Parliament. As details of the plan were debated by politicians and the public, it became clear that between the choices of remaining in the EU or leaving it, there were many distinct alternatives. People began to talk about Soft Brexit and Hard Brexit, and each of those options had several variants. Who was going to decide? After it had repeatedly rejected May's plan, Parliament was presented with eight alternatives, none of which got the support of a majority. Despite being forced to seek a compromise with the Labour Party, May appeared unwilling to shift her position for fear of splitting her party. Given the scale of disagreement, arguments arose: no matter what decision the politicians arrived at, it must be put to a popular vote once more. But that was only begging the question of what would happen if the people voted down the decision. Would it be back to square one?

The Brexit fiasco reveals, among other things, the severe lack of correspondence between the positions adopted by the major political parties, with their long-established procedures for choosing leaders and declaring policy, and the opinion of the people. How could a gap of such magnitude emerge within a system of representative democracy that had hitherto proved to be so adaptive and resilient? One reason is suggested by my analysis in chapter 2 of the immensely complex and interconnected structures of decision-making that have emerged in advanced capitalist countries tying together the government, financial institutions, the market, and civil society organizations. These decisions aspire to take into account not only the objective facts that define various alternative choices but also such intangible elements as psychological proclivities and sentiments that affect market or electoral outcomes. The rationalizing thrust of calculative reasoning has shaped these structures to facilitate optimal decision-making by experts who are presumed to be free from ideological prejudices. Could such a complex array of interconnected decisions ever be encapsulated within a simple yes or no choice in a popular referendum?

The question raised by Brexit concerns the very locus of sovereignty; that is the measure of the hegemonic crisis. Writing in the middle of another pervasive crisis of parliamentary democracy nearly a century ago, Carl Schmitt made a perceptive observation:

> Every concrete juristic decision contains a moment of indifference from the perspective of content, because the juristic deduction is not traceable in the last detail to its premises and because the circumstance that requires a decision remains an independently determining moment. . . . The certainty of the decision is, from the perspective of sociology, of particular interest in an age of intense commercial activity because in numerous cases commerce is less concerned with a particular content than with a calculable certainty.[1]

Schmitt, of course, concluded from this that the legal force of a decision emanated from the competence of the sovereign authority that had issued it and was "independent of the correctness of its content."[2] Which was the competent sovereign authority to decide on Brexit? The leader of an elected government, in an act of inexplicable hubris, had suddenly pronounced, "Let the people decide." When the people did, even if by the narrowest of margins, it fell on the government to negotiate with the European authorities the legal and technical modalities of the separation. But the government's plan would have to be turned into law by Parliament, the sovereign law-making authority. When the plan failed to muster a majority in Parliament, the government could only appeal to the EU to give it more time to come up with a different plan. But the EU had already negotiated a plan with a government that represented a sovereign state! And now, even if Parliament were to decide on a new plan, would it not be necessary to take it to the people once more in order to make the decision legitimate? Schmitt, the most consummate philosopher of antiliberal authoritarian government, would not have been surprised to witness this comical predicament of divided sovereignty. Liberals, he would have said, try to solve the problem of sovereignty by suppressing it. But now that the comfortable shelter of the integral state has collapsed, where does liberal democracy find the decision-making authority that is both legally competent and morally legitimate?

In France the established party system had come apart at the time of the presidential elections of May 2017. Emmanuel Macron, a young centrist supporter of globalization and the EU, ran for election as head of La République En Marche!, a party he had founded only a few months earlier; he won by defeating Marine le Pen, the leader of the extreme right-wing Front National (now renamed Rassemblement National). The traditional centrist and socialist parties were left straggling far behind. It was an astonishingly quick upending of the party system, probably unprecedented in its scope and speed in any Western democracy in the postwar era (though, as we have seen, it has happened on several occasions in politics in Indian states). Yet Macron was no populist demagogue. He attempted to project the virtues of balanced judgment, rational policy-making, technical efficiency, and international cooperation in a world threatened by angry extremists.

The Gilets Jaunes (Yellow Vests) movement began across several French cities in November 2018 following an online campaign against a hike in the fuel tax. As it gained steam, as many as 300,000 demonstrators were said to have gathered every weekend in the winter months, wearing the signature yellow vests of motorists, most protesting peacefully but some smashing shop windows, setting fire to cars, and clashing with the police. The protests were particularly strong in the provincial towns, where there was great resentment against the glittering prosperity of the big cities while people in the peripheries struggled to cope with high taxes, poor services, and paltry incomes. The government began to feel the pressure. It responded along two lines: cracking down hard on violent protests while opening channels of consultation and compromise. Protesters were met with tear gas and rubber bullets; there were few fatalities but numerous serious injuries. But the government also announced that the tax increases and rise in electricity prices would be put on hold and that the minimum wage would be raised. Since it was difficult to negotiate with a leaderless and horizontally organized movement, a series of public debates, eventually numbering over ten thousand, were organized around the country at which ordinary people could air their grievances in the presence of government officials. By April 2019 public support for the movement, which at its peak had reached nearly 40 percent of those polled, was said to have fallen in the major cities, although it was still holding up in rural areas.

The Gilets Jaunes movement fits with our characterization of populist opposition movements—except in one important respect. It has drawn support across the political spectrum, with many participants having earlier voted for the far-right Marine le Pen and others for the radical-left Jean-Luc Mélenchon. These seemingly disparate groups came together in demanding a series of measures to ameliorate the economic difficulties of those outside the metropolitan enclaves of affluence. When the government claimed that the fuel tax was an environmental measure, the protesters countered by pointing out that a flat tax would punish the poor rather than deter those who did most of the polluting. What the movement did not have was a leader, and it steadfastly rejected a vertical organization, preferring instead to gather and consult principally through online social media. Notably though, a focus was provided for the floating signifier of the enemy in the figure of *le roi Macron*, the tyrant king who had to be symbolically decapitated. It is significant that, following several concessions by the government on economic demands, the movement has tended to hone in on a single major political slogan: Macron must go!

Invocations of 1789 are also significant. An online list of "people's directives" was created in which laws could be proposed and voted on by adding signatures; if a proposal got more than 700,000 signatures, it would go to the National Assembly, where it could be turned into law and put to a popular referendum. The massive collection of testimonies at the thousands of local meetings that constituted the "great national debate" called for by Macron is being called the *cahiers de doléances* (book of complaints), after a similar collection ordered by Louis XVI days before the French Revolution.[3] There is, as in all populist movements, an excess of egalitarian imprecision that, as I have explained in chapter 3 in the context of Laclau's definition of populism, is its strength rather than its weakness. Nevertheless, the energy and resilience of this leaderless movement across France has surprised most observers.

There are important similarities in the social background of those in Britain who voted for Brexit and the Gilets Jaunes in France. Voters in favor of leaving the EU came mostly from old industrial and rural British counties where average incomes are low, unemployment is high, and educational qualifications are insufficient for good jobs. Voters in favor of retaining EU membership tended to be from London and other flourishing urban areas, were better educated, and belonged to the upper middle classes (in addition to the people of Scotland and Northern Ireland, a majority of whom voted to stay). In France the demonstrators are from regions of deprivation; they are generally older, less educated, and feel left out of the new arenas of economic opportunity. This confirms a general feature of popular agitations in Western capitalist countries: They mirror a widely perceived disparity in incomes, opportunities, and future expectations, between those who are able to enter the metropolitan enclaves of prosperity and those consigned to the crumbling peripheries.[4] In Britain, voters in favor of Brexit are particularly resentful of new immigrants from eastern Europe who, unlike the earlier wave of migrants from the former colonies, are threatening to take away jobs from the local working class. Also significant is that unlike the periodic race riots in Britain or the insurrections in the banlieues inhabited by poor immigrants in France, the mobilizations have not included immigrant populations at all. The populist upsurge excludes the culturally marginal; it claims to re-create the authentic people-nation.

The Populist Moment

Chantal Mouffe has identified the hegemonic crisis that has gripped Western democracies as a populist moment. Following Laclau's analysis, Mouffe argues that the sheer multiplicity of heterogeneous unfulfilled demands has destabilized established structures of rule. The opposition to the prevailing order is not coming from any particular group or class, nor is it restricted to an identifiable ideological formation. The interregnum created by the crisis has opened up the possibility for the appearance of "the people" as a new political subject.[5]

But there are, Mouffe says, two populist tendencies contending with each other. Right-wing populism emphasizes *national* sovereignty as one constituted by "true nationals"; it is majoritarian and xenophobic. By contrast, left-wing populism speaks of *popular* sovereignty and stresses equality and social justice. Left-wing populism holds the promise of a hegemonic strategy upholding democracy as the key discursive modality that would produce "the people" as a new political subject. Rejecting the neoliberal consensus of an apolitical surrender to the market, left-wing populism must uphold the civic republican virtue of active popular participation in sovereignty.[6] Crucially, it must appreciate the political force of affective ties that hold together a people in a collective body such as the nation.

Although Mouffe refers to movements such as Podemos in Spain and Syriza in Greece, her description of left-wing populism is more programmatic than an account of an actual political tendency. But a careful examination of Mouffe's proposal shows that her intended programmatic goal cannot be reached unless the movement transcends populism. Here is why.

We have seen that bourgeois hegemony was achieved under the welfare state through a long-term pedagogical project of producing the citizen-subject with social rights. This was transformed by neoliberalism through another pedagogical project, producing a consumer-subject who could be induced to respond to incentives and penalties. The result, as Mouffe correctly claims, was an evacuation of politics and widespread apathy among voters. This was the moment when populist movements and leaders tried to invoke the forgotten tradition of popular political initiative. But populism, as we have seen in numerous instances, is necessarily confined to a series of tactical battles; it does not have the capacity to forge a sustained hegemonic strategy of creating a new political subject. The crucial problem is that in order to mobilize the resources for implementing its policies of social justice, populist regimes have to depend on revenues collected from profitable capitalist enterprises. Hence, the viability of populist regimes become tied to the continued profitability of the existing corporate manufacturing and financial sectors. Populism cannot have a strategy to transform the structures of property or production.

Although Mouffe claims that left-wing populism will be anticapitalist, not by privileging the working class but because there are many points of antagonism between capital and various sections of the people, she incorrectly assumes that the demobilization and scattering of the working class in Western capitalist societies today applies equally to the capitalist class.[7] That is not true. In fact, the owners of capital constitute the only fundamental class that is fully conscious of its interests and possesses the organization to act politically across every nation-state in North America and western Europe. Never was this better demonstrated than in the way it acted to preserve itself during and after the financial crisis of 2008–2009.

Overcoming the Financial Crisis

What began with the bursting of a speculative bubble in the subprime housing market in the United States turned into a fullblown crisis in September 2008 when Fannie Mae and Freddie Mac, two major mortgage banks, had to be taken over by the federal government. A week later, the giant investment firm Lehman Brothers went bankrupt, leading to a crash in the stock market and jeopardizing the entire financial system. Soon, given the deep involvement of European banks in the US subprime mortgage market, the shock waves carried across the Atlantic. Ben Bernanke, then chair of the Federal Reserve, later described the financial crisis of September–October 2008 as the worst in global history, including the Great Depression.[8]

In his masterly reconstruction of the crisis and its aftermath, Adam Tooze points out that in the global financial system, whose central axis runs between the United States and Europe, there are only between twenty and thirty banks that really matter. If one includes nationally significant banks, there would be at most a hundred financial firms of consequence in the entire world. They are known in the business as "systemically important financial institutions."[9] These banks, and the people who run them, control a highly centralized network that wields far greater power over the lives of people than do most nation-states. The scale of global financialization, for instance, is far bigger than the volume of global trade. Also significant is the fact that the dollar remains the liquidity provider of last resort in the global banking system. The crisis and its handling revealed in no uncertain terms that the European Central Bank had become thoroughly Americanized (18).

From September 2008 onward, as the crisis unfolded, the leaders of global finance demanded massive and decisive state intervention, as though it was a military emergency, in order to save the industry. They got what they wanted. Tooze remarks that the crisis was "met with a mobilization of state action without precedent in the history of capitalism" (165–66). Led by Bernanke, president of the New York Federal Reserve Timothy Geithner, and Secretary of the Treasury Henry Paulson, key figures from Wall Street were brought together with top political leaders, including President George W. Bush and Democratic Party presidential contender Barack Obama, to urge immediate action by government. When the Republican-controlled House of Representatives refused to pass legislation to set up the Troubled Assets Relief Program (TARP), with conservative members arguing that this would lead to nationalization of private enterprises, leaders of finance went into overdrive, warning that if government did not act immediately, the United States might be left without an economy in a matter of days. TARP was passed. Using a combination of massive loans to banks, recapitalization, asset purchases, and state guarantees of bank deposits, a total of $1 trillion was spent by the government to stabilize the financial system. Major automobile companies, including Chrysler and General Motors, were given bailouts. The Federal Reserve reduced the lending rate to zero.

Even more indicative of the power and determination of the leaders of finance capital to secure their interests was the way the Federal Reserve acted to bail out the European Central Bank when it ran into serious trouble in 2009. The existence of so-called swap lines that allowed dollar bonds to be redesignated into euros or sterling, and vice versa, meant that a currency crisis could be avoided in Europe because of the support of the dollar. But more significantly, says Tooze, massive funds were actually provided by the Federal Reserve to European banks without informing the public and without explicit political authorization (215). Considerations of democratic transparency were apparently irrelevant when it involved the serious matter of stabilizing the markets. As Jean-Claude Juncker of Luxembourg, then the Eurogroup chair, remarked after being caught lying about a meeting between top American and European bankers, "I am for secret, dark debates. . . . I'm ready to be insulted as being insufficiently democratic, but I want to be serious . . . when it becomes serious, you have to lie."[10]

The owners of capital in the United States and the major countries of Europe did not constitute a homogeneous bloc; there were many divergences in interests and stakes. But unequal power relations and the spirit of solidarity and compromise enabled them to make crucial decisions that would ultimately pull them out of the crisis. Thus, the determination of German chancellor Angela Merkel not to offend voters who did not want to pay for a Greek bailout prevailed in Europe's decision to force the Syriza government to accept a brutal austerity plan, even though the rational solution would have been to restructure its loans. Relations between the American and European players were not always smooth. Besides, China also emerged as a crucial player. In a series of explicit acts of cooperation, fiscal and financial stimulus policies adopted by China in 2009 helped overcome the global crisis. It was not necessarily the technocrats who always won out; a robust understanding of politics and ideology was part of the consciousness that guided the actions of the leaders of the capitalist class at this moment of crisis. As Tooze explains, "Political choice, ideology and agency are everywhere across this narrative with highly consequential results."[11]

Popular Initiative

The possibilities of left-wing populist movements like Italy's Movimento 5 Stelle, Spain's Podemos, or Greece's Syriza to win elections, join governments, and steer decisions in a direction more favorable to the needs of ordinary people are not to be scoffed at. They can also play an important role in keeping at bay the hateful and violent politics of right-wing populists. But they cannot transcend the inherent limits of populist politics. They will continue to depend on a charismatic leader at the top of a centralized organization and inevitably veer in the direction of using arbitrary and authoritarian power, ostensibly to deliver justice to the people. They will also be mindful of ensuring that markets are not disturbed, since only a steady flow of revenues from business would finance their social expenditure. Given those limits, left-wing populism in itself cannot mount a long-term strategy of hegemonic transformation.

It is also important to note that the deep crisis that has unsettled long-standing economic and political structures in Western capitalist countries has produced far more radical responses from the Right than it has from the Left. Right-wing populists have been willing to run roughshod over legal and constitutional rules, democratic conventions, and institutional norms to gain partisan advantage. They have successfully put into the public sphere a new narrative of nationalism that rejects the liberal idea of civic membership and instead redefines the nation-state as constituted exclusively by a culturally authentic people-nation, specifically targeting culturally alien immigrants as enemies. Potentially, this represents a long-term pedagogic project that seeks to achieve hegemony. Combined with the fact that their tactical battles are intended to facilitate centralized, authoritarian and arbitrary rule, there is little doubt that right-wing populists have embarked on a strategy of reconstituting Western capitalist societies on an alarmingly different basis.

By contrast, left-wing populists have shown that they have far greater stakes in the existing system and have proposed little beyond the promise of a return to the happy days of social democracy and multiculturalism. As we have seen, when given a chance to run governments they have been hobbled by their inability to break through established institutional norms and challenge the structures of economic dominance. They have been unable to produce an emotionally powerful narrative tying the people-nation to the nation-state that can counter the right-wing version of nationalism. A different possibility does exist in a grassroots populist movement such as the Gilets Jaunes if it remains oppositional and resists the temptation to turn itself into an electoral party. There are signs that, in a matter of months, the movement has managed to introduce several new institutional procedures to make the government accountable to the people without the mediation of party representatives. One could imagine this to be what Antonio Gramsci called a strategy of molecular transformation—a long-term effort in the war of position. But that is something that, at least at this moment, lies in an unknown future.

Inevitably, therefore, one must return to the Gramscian question: Which social force can craft a hegemonic strategy that goes beyond the tactical battles of populism to lay the foundations for a significant social transformation? When only one fundamental social class—the owners of capital—is well organized and self-conscious and the others are demobilized and scattered, where are we to find the agency for a counterhegemonic struggle? Before I answer that final question, let me review the situation in the postcolonial world.

The New Fault Line

Let me begin by hazarding a somewhat wild hypothesis on the basis of my analysis of populist politics in India. Capitalist development in countries like India that are characterized as emerging economies has produced a new fault line along which increasingly massive battles are being waged. If we allow the use of an old-fashioned dialectical language, we might even say that a new contradiction has appeared. Instead of the contradiction between the traditional and modern sectors of the economy or that between capital and labor, the new contradiction is between the formally regulated economic sphere dominated by corporate capital and driven by the logic of accumulation and the vast and widening expanse of the so-called informal economy, fully embedded in market relations but reproduced primarily by the logic of satisfying subsistence needs. The emergence of this contradiction has brought about significant changes in the strategies of the passive revolution carried out on behalf of the owners of capital. As far as the formally organized economy is concerned, technological innovation, the utilization of suitable export markets, stronger links with global financial networks, and, needless to say, a suitably favorable regulatory and tax regime are expected to ensure the conditions of capital accumulation—if all goes well, at a growth rate of 10 percent or higher every year. Nearly everyone involved in the formal economy stands to benefit from this growth. Not only the owners of capital and managerial personnel but even workers and other employees involved in production, sales, and other services receive a share—albeit an unequal one—of the gains. The result is that at each level of the employment structure the incomes of owners, managers, and workers in the formal sector are significantly, and increasingly, higher than those in the informal sector.

There are two political consequences. First, the argument can be made, and powerfully propagated through the media controlled by corporate capital, that rapid growth of the formal sector is the secure way to create employment and incomes that will, by trickling downward and outward through ancillary producers and service providers, boost the economy in general. Second, and conversely, the growing and visible inequality between incomes and lifestyles at all levels in the formal and informal sectors, not to mention the already unviable traditional sector, can give rise to the opposite argument: that the rapid growth of the formal sector leads to biased and unjust results, enriching only a tiny section consisting of the urban middle class and the organized working class while causing misery to millions who have been ousted from their traditional livelihoods and desperately seek to find subsistence in the overcrowded informal sector. These two opposed political consequences have together created the new contradiction.

In what sense is it new? If we follow Kalyan Sanyal's reasoning, primitive accumulation in today's postcolonial economies cannot be understood within the old model of transition from a traditional agrarian economy to a modern industrial one. The growth of the formal economy does indeed require the acquisition of agricultural land for factories, townships, roads, airports, etc., causing the displacement of vast numbers of traditional farmers and artisans and a general decline of traditional occupations. But the conditions of accumulation in the formal economy can accommodate only a tiny fraction of this dispossessed population as wage workers. Most are left to fend for themselves in the informal economy. The latter is not a vestige of the traditional economy, however; it is a creation of capitalist growth. Indeed, the faster the growth of the formal sector, the greater the density as well as the spread of the informal sector. Thus, the historicist narrative of a gradual transition from the traditional agrarian economy to a modern industrial one does not hold. The informal economy is a thoroughly modern organization of enterprise and labor functioning within the given market conditions. Its key difference from the formal economy is that it is able to reproduce itself only because enterprises operate merely to ensure subsistence and not to accumulate capital for further growth; it also receives crucial support, elicited through political pressure, from the state to maintain those subsistence levels. The state is able to provide these subsistence benefits to the urban and rural poor by spending a part of the revenues generated from the formal sector in various schemes of poverty removal. This defines a new modality of the passive revolution of capital in postcolonial countries. The owners of capital can legitimize their dominance over the entire economy only by allowing the governmental institutions of the state to act as a mediating agency to enable the dispossessed poor to survive.

It is not as if the contradiction between capital and labor disappears. The existence of a vast pool of unemployed laborers acts as a downward pull on wage rates in the formal sector, even though the use of increasingly sophisticated technology also has the opposite effect of creating a need for workers with higher education and technical skills. But the structural opposition between owners of capital and sellers of labor power persists at the workplace. The fact that workers in the formal sector also have legally established rights to organize, make demands, and negotiate with management enables them to press their employers for better wages, working conditions, benefits, etc. Yet the commonly shared knowledge that employment in the formal sector pays far better and is more secure than the precarious conditions of life in the informal economy fosters a strong interest of workers in the well-being and growth of the enterprise and the formal sector as a whole. A job in a corporate enterprise comes to be seen as an opportunity for social mobility into the middle class. The prosperity of those within the corporate sector, as well as the aspiration to enter it on the part of those outside it, serves to bolster the hegemony of corporate capital over urban middle-class society. In fact, unlike the developmentalist decades after Indian independence, when the state sector led the economy, government employment now tails the corporate sector in terms of prestige. To use once again an old-fashioned language, the contradiction between capital and labor in the formal sector, or between managers and employees in the public sector, becomes a secondary one in comparison with that between the formal and state sectors as a whole and the informal. The latter is the principal contradiction of our time.

Admittedly, this is a crude summary of an immensely complex and rapidly changing situation. Further, there are considerable variations across regions and sectors that qualify whether, or to what extent, the hypothesis works as an explanation of current economic and political tendencies. Nevertheless, my hypothesis is no cruder than the slogans of many powerful populist movements today that are symptomatic of the underlying fault line I have described herein.

What are the claims and achievements of the many populist regimes that have appeared in different Indian states in the last four decades? Some features are common. Thus, in urban areas, administrative arrangements are usually made to selectively protect slums from demolition or provide suitable rehabilitation if slums have to be cleared for infrastructure development projects; street peddlers are allowed to ply their trade; violation of labor or pollution laws by small-scale production and service units is condoned. In rural areas, small farmers are sometimes protected from losing their land, agricultural loans are waived, and subsidized water and electricity are provided for agriculture. The government often announces a minimum support price for certain agricultural commodities; if the market price falls below the announced price, government agencies step in to buy the product from farmers. This involves a careful balancing act between ensuring a reasonable return to farmers and an affordable price for poor urban consumers. Most Indian state governments supply subsidized food grains to both urban and rural poor and free meals to rural schoolchildren. Schemes that achieve popularity in one state are quickly replicated in others. Thus, the scheme to supply rice to the poor at two rupees per kilogram, first launched by N. T. Rama Rao in the 1980s, has become so emblematic of a government that cares for the poor that it has not only been adopted by most Indian states but, three decades later, the price has stayed at two rupees. Repeated agitation from farmers has led to one state government after another announcing waivers on outstanding bank loans, even though most experts agree that this measure does not benefit poor farmers, since they usually borrow from private moneylenders, and it clearly reduces the incentive to pay back bank loans.

What is significant in all of these schemes of governmental populism, as well as in the political rhetoric that is used to justify and celebrate them, is that they exclude from their scope not only the urban middle class but also the workers in the formal sector: these population groups are not regarded as deserving the special attention of government. For instance, a scheme for subsidizing liquefied petroleum cooking gas for domestic use, which was once universally available, was a few years ago restricted only to poor families because more affluent consumers were now expected to pay market prices. Government benefits of this kind are now increasingly justified by the populist language of helping the poor rather than the universalist language of social welfare. The situation has clearly changed greatly from that of the 1950s and 1960s, when government support of this kind was primarily directed at the urban middle class as well as the urban poor, who were dependent on the vagaries of market shortages and inflationary pressures; the rural population was regarded as belonging to a traditional agrarian economy that produced its own subsistence needs. Today the fault line between the formal and informal sectors, as well as the fact that the latter is not a traditional sector but fully located within the market, are reflected in the policies and slogans of Indian populism.

This gives rise to two alternative strategies of rule. The first follows the logic of selectively satisfying differential demands while optimizing expected costs and benefits, breaking up target populations, and discouraging mass consolidation of demands. This strategy fits in well with the neoliberal prescription for development (i.e., to promote rapid growth of the formal sector and thus keep civil society happy) while managing political society through the differential use of neoliberal tactics. To be successful, the strategy requires the assistance of the state in negotiating suitable international trade and financial connections for private capital to find export markets and funds for investment. This carries the danger of exposing an often unbalanced economy to the vicissitudes of the global commodities and financial markets. Of course, a new option has opened up for many African and Asian countries in the form of infrastructure assistance and large loans from China. The political implications of this option are as yet unclear. It is also a strategy that must depend heavily on experts to constantly balance, through a complex deployment of technical instruments, the often conflicting requirements of bureaucratic rationality, legal validation, fiscal prudence, and political legitimacy. But the intended effect of the strategy is to conceal the fault line between the prosperous world of the formal economy and civil society and the precarious terrain of the informal economy and political society.

The first strategy could, however, meet with a populist opposition that successfully establishes chains of equivalence between the many disparate population groups that feel aggrieved because their demands have not been met. An internal border is then created between the oppressor elite and the oppressed people: the former becomes the enemy of the latter. As I have shown above, populist governmental policies serve to define this internal border such that it largely coincides with the fault line between the formal and informal sectors or—what is more or less the same thing—between civil and political society. When a populist movement comes to power, it must continue to rhetorically perform the presence of the contradiction, for otherwise it runs the risk of diluting its populist image. Even as it necessarily adopts many of the neoliberal tactics of satisfying demands according to the logic of difference, a successful populist regime manages to fill in the floating signifiers of "the people" and "the enemy" with fresh content in order to stay relevant to the most perceptible dividing line separating the haves from the have-nots. As we have seen, this is most often accomplished by personalizing sovereign power in a popularly anointed leader who rules with arbitrary and authoritarian powers. Yet expenditure on populist schemes has to be met from revenues generated mainly by the organized sector. Hence, even as populist regimes loudly condemn the corrupt rich and seek to extract—both legally and through political coercion—funds from the corporate sector, they also have a stake in the flourishing of that sector. The strategy of populist rule, then, is one in which the internal border between the people and its enemy is rhetorically dramatized, even magnified, and state support is provided to the poor to help maintain their subsistence, but no attempt is made to curtail or challenge the structure of dominance of corporate capital. Thus, even though it is a risky option with many imponderables, populism could also become a strategy of the passive revolution of capital. What it certainly is not is a counterhegemonic resistance to the rule of capital.

Dangers and Opportunities

Nonetheless, by loudly emphasizing the rift between the elite and the masses, populist politics in postcolonial democracies does renew the forgotten promise of popular sovereignty. In its relatively benign form, it acknowledges the moral duty of a democratic government to ensure that the poor have the minimum means of subsistence and agrees to negotiate selective and often exceptional terms of benefit with population groups in what I have called political society. But its darker side is the legitimacy that is conferred on violent displays of popular anger as a tactic of democratic politics. Analyzing "India's illiberal democracy," Thomas Hansen has pointed out how "vernacular publics" have promoted a popular politics of passion and anger such that violence has become "the general equivalent of India's multiple publics." The depth and intensity of a popular agitation is frequently measured by the scale of violence it brings about on both the part of the agitators and the agencies of law enforcement. "The mightiest socio-political force in India today," explains Hansen, "is neither the state nor the law but deeply embedded vernacular ideas of popular sovereignty." What Hansen means by vernacular publics are precisely collective forms of expression of popular demands that are not framed by the legal and constitutional rules of association followed in civil society. Hansen also notes that these publics are not the same as traditional caste or religious communities; rather, they stand for "the people" (*janata* in Hindi), which is a more open and not preestablished category that needs to be filled in and performed in order to be potent.[12] Political action in the name of popular sovereignty has thus come to include publicly mobilized violence as a tactic of democracy.

Since populism harps on the divide between the elite ensconced within a flourishing civil society and the miserable masses struggling to survive in the informal economy and yet has neither a counterhegemonic strategy nor a pedagogical project, it opens up historic possibilities, some of which are hopeful and others dangerous. Here are some of them.

When populist movements and leaders realize that they cannot attack the existing structure of dominance of corporate capital and yet must keep alive the confrontation between the people and its enemy, they could direct popular anger against a more accessible and vulnerable target. A common move is to mobilize a majority based on ethnicity, region, or even partisan affiliation against a minority group that is allegedly corrupting the people-nation or conspiring against the nation-state. The signifiers known as the people and the enemy are suitably filled with content that dramatizes the conflict by giving it a histori-cal narrative and offering a radical solution such as expulsion or demotion to an inferior grade of citizenship. Thus, the regime of Recep Tayyip Erdoğan in Turkey has often targeted the Kurds as a threat to the people-nation and, following the attempted coup against Erdoğan in 2016, has carried out a drastic purge of the bureaucracy, the judiciary, educational institutions, and the news media to supposedly cleanse them of supporters of the exiled cleric Fethullah Gülen, who is alleged to be the leader of a giant conspiracy against the nation-state. The Awami League regime in Bangladesh characterizes the opposition Bangladesh Nationalist Party as historically committed to the subversion of the people-nation and hence undeserving of the liberal entitle-ments of electoral democracy. The Bharatiya Janata Party and its affiliated Hindu organizations in India question the loyalty of the Muslim minority and threaten to complete the suppos-edly unfinished business of the partition of the country. The military in Myanmar, following sustained agitation by fiercely nationalist Buddhist monks, has physically expelled tens of thousands of minority Rohingya Muslims, and the demo-cratically elected government of Aung San Suu Kyi has pas-sively endorsed the policy. The popular resentment against dis-parity and deprivation is thus turned into angry attacks on behalf of a majority—the authentic people-nation—against its enemy, the minority other.

The response of civil society led by the propertied and pre-dominantly urban middle class to populist electoral politics can take two forms. The relatively benign form of governmental populism, while it is not celebrated, is for the most part tolerated by civil society as the price that must be paid for securing political legitimacy for the growing affluence of the numerical minority that constitutes the corporate and state sectors. I have described this as the first strategy of the passive revolution in postcolonial democracies today. But when a populist regime becomes arbitrary and authoritarian, and tramples on civic freedoms and institutional norms in order to satisfy popular demands, civil society makes up for its deficiency in the electoral arena by seeking the intervention of the courts of law. If this fails, however, the urban propertied classes organized in civil society may turn against electoral democracy itself, usually with the help of the armed forces. The passive revolution then moves into an unpredictable and dangerous terrain where overt coercion rather than persuasion becomes the modality of rule. The early twenty-first century has seen several such instances—most notably, the ouster of two consecutive popularly elected governments by the army in Thailand and the violent termination of the elected Muslim Brotherhood government, followed by the reestablishment of military rule, in Egypt. In Brazil, urban civil society, the courts, and the military elite seem to have acted in concert to dislodge from power the populist Workers' Party and prevent its leader, Luiz Inácio Lula da Silva, from contesting the elections.

What are the possibilities of counterhegemonic initiatives on behalf of the subaltern classes? The frequent invocations from populist parties and leaders of the sanctity of popular sovereignty, even though such invocations may be thoroughly insincere, must surely spark efforts to mobilize mass energies for a lasting transformation of an oppressive order. What is significant in this respect is the spectacular spread of digital technology and social media in many countries of Africa and Asia and its effects in the political domain. The unprecedented 2011 mobilization in Cairo's Tahrir Square, and indeed the entire phenomenon called the Arab Spring, has been linked to the availability of this novel instrument of swift communication within expanding networks that need not depend on traditional party organizations. Since then, popular agitations over various issues in several countries have been mounted with the help of social media. Many such movements have lacked organization and recognized structures of leadership. Should the apparent spontaneity of inspiration and nonhierarchical mode of collective action that characterize these movements not be seen as harbingers of a new, as yet undefined, form of popular counter-hegemonic politics?

Before we jump to quick conclusions, we must consider the reasons why social media has facilitated certain kinds of mobilizations rather than others. First, its format makes false news indistinguishable from validated information. If we remember the role played by rumor in older forms of political agitation, there was a clear distinction between the mode of circulation of rumor from that of authenticated news: rumor had greater force in networks that either did not have access to news or did not trust the agencies that put it out. Now the same source doles out both kinds of content with no distinguishing marks. Second, social media tends to magnify content that strikes extreme emotional registers. As such, sensational and provocative content has far greater circulation than does genuine news. Once again, the older distinction between newspapers of repute and the tabloid press has been obliterated. Third, the filtering mechanism of social media deliberately creates narrow echo chambers where people with similar opinions talk to one another. The result is that the gradations introduced over several decades in public discourse by editorialized print literature and news media have been swept away by social media technology and the new television news channels that seek to duplicate the same echo chambers. As Siva Vaidhyanathan, who has studied the phenomenon, remarks, "Sophistry is the dominant cultural practice of the moment.... The very institutions we have carefully constructed and maintained to filter out nonsense and noise and to forge consensus of thought and action are withering."[13]

The obvious retort to this observation would be to point out that those filters were put in place precisely to secure the conditions of reproduction of the existing structure of political power. In other words, using Gramscian terminology, the editorially policed discourse of the public sphere is an essential part of the hegemony of the propertied classes over civil society and, wherever possible, a key instrument of the integral state of the passive revolution. Should counterhegemonic efforts at mobilizing popular opposition not try to bypass or subvert those hegemonic protocols?

By placing the problem on the Gramscian terrain of hegemonic strategy and counterstrategy, we gain a clearer perspective on the challenges that must be faced by any effort today to assert popular sovereignty in postcolonial countries. We have seen that even the most powerful populist mobilizations in these countries have not achieved anything beyond a series of tactical blows aimed at extracting benefits for poor and marginal populations. It is true that corporate capital and the propertied classes, faced with the threat of populist agitation, have been forced to yield to some extent. But, paradoxically, the ability of populist regimes to continue to deliver such benefits to its supporters crucially depends on the sustained prosperity of the corporate sector. Hence, populism comes to develop a stake in the perpetuation of the existing structure of property ownership and social production.

While social media based on digital technology is celebrated for the unprecedented access it affords ordinary people to large anonymous public networks of communication, its structure of ownership and managerial control consists of a few gigantic corporations larger in size than any seen in the history of capitalism. Apple, Facebook, Google, and Microsoft are among the largest companies in the world today, doing business in every country and testing the powers of every sovereign state to rein in their irresistible sway over the space of public conversation. They have grown big not through competition but by resisting it. As Peter Thiel, the founder of PayPal, has put it, "Capitalism and competition are opposites. Capitalism is premised on the accumulation of capital, but under perfect competition, all profits get competed away. The lesson for entrepreneurs is clear . . . competition is for losers."[14]

Even as there have been numerous instances in many countries of the lethal use of social media to spread hateful and usually false information against specific groups or individuals, thus often leading to mob violence and killings, social media giants are reluctant to accept responsibility for acting as the carrier of such harmful messages and, by using the unprecedented power of their technology and business organization over the daily lives of millions of people in every country, are resisting efforts by state authorities to question their claim to impunity. Is it conceivable that if sustained political campaigns are launched over social media that seriously threaten to upset existing structures of property and power, those giant global corporations would magnanimously allow their technologies to be used for their own destruction? A century and a half ago, Karl Marx identified a dynamic by which, with increased concentration and centralization of productive forces at the industrial workplace, workers—the true creators of value—would acquire the potential to seize the entire process of social production from the hands of capitalists. The prophecy did not materialize. It seems impossible to conceive of a dynamic by which the vast multitudes who communicate through digital media could seize control of its technology and organization.

Counterhegemony and Transformation

What, then, remains of the possibility of counterhegemonic transformation? I have a twofold answer.

First, the mobilizations by left-wing populists to win elections and enter government in order to promote policies that might alleviate the desperate conditions of life of poorer sections of the people are indeed worthy of support. In Western countries, such mobilizations will highlight the glaring inequalities that the latest phase of capitalist accumulation has produced. In postcolonial countries, the divide between the formal economy and urban civil society, on the one hand, and the informal economy and political society, on the other, will mark the internal border between the people and their enemy. Nevertheless, the limits of such populist mobilization must be recognized and the dangers they carry of a descent into corrupt authoritarianism borne in mind. Populism cannot become transformative without transcending itself.

Second, there must, then, be a more long-term project of producing, circulating, and instilling in the popular consciousness a narrative of social transformation. In particular, the challenge posed by right-wing populism, which is prepared to trample over liberal institutions and mount a visceral nationalist counternarrative, cannot be met by electoral tactics alone. Of course, this is easier said than done. But saying is the first step toward doing. The project must proceed from a sustained critique of existing institutions and practices of power. Some of the elements of this critique, inasmuch as they relate to global networks of trade and finance, information, military power, and diplomatic alliances, will be common to most countries. But other aspects of the critique must deal more specifically with the varying conditions of inequality and exploitation in advanced capitalist economies as opposed to developing countries. An important lesson of the populist moment, however, is that rational critique of mistaken and harmful policies is not sufficient for the mobilization of democratic opinion. What is necessary is an alternative narrative with the emotional power to draw people into collective political action. I have argued that a new relation between the people-nation and the nation-state, appropriate for the present moment of hegemonic crisis, must be imagined and turned into a pedagogical project. Needless to say, this narrative will be different for each country.

Who will begin this counterhegemonic project? Critique, imagination, and pedagogy are part of the intellectual's calling. As Gramsci's notebooks continue to remind us, intellectuals who are able to turn their ideas into the stuff of popular education lay the groundwork for hegemonic transformation. Those are my words of optimism for the readers of this gloomy book.

NOTES

1. Even Justice

1. Ruth Benedict, *The Chrysanthemum and the Sword: Patterns of Japanese Culture* (1946; Boston: Houghton Mifflin, 2006).
2. For a retelling of this story, see Madhusree Mukerjee, *Churchill's Secret War: The British Empire and the Ravaging of India During World War II* (Boston: Basic Books, 2011).
3. Margaret M. Caffrey, *Ruth Benedict: Stranger in This Land* (Austin: University of Texas Press, 1989), 319–21.
4. Margaret Mead, *Ruth Benedict* (New York: Columbia University Press, 1972), 64.
5. Caffrey, *Ruth Benedict*, 326; Judith Schachter Modell, *Ruth Benedict: Patterns of a Life* (Philadelphia: University of Pennsylvania Press, 1984), 292. Mead's own account of the research project is in Mead, *Ruth Benedict*, 65–75.
6. See Benedict, *The Chrysanthemum*, especially 222–23. Hereafter, page numbers will be cited parenthetically in the text.
7. Louis Dumont, *Homo Hierarchicus: The Caste System and Its Implications* (Chicago: University of Chicago Press, 1970); Louis Dumont, *From Mandeville to Marx: The Genesis and Triumph of Economic Ideology* (Chicago: University of Chicago Press, 1977).

8. Richard H. Minear, *Victors' Justice: The Tokyo War Crimes Trial* (Princeton, N.J.: Princeton University Press, 1971), 26–33. This was the first critical academic study of the Tokyo trial in the West.

9. The lectures were published as Radhabinod Pal, *Crimes in International Relations* (Calcutta: University of Calcutta, 1955). The dissenting judgment is Radhabinod Pal, *International Military Tribunal for the Far East: Dissentient Judgment of Justice Pal* (Tokyo: Kokusho-Kankokai, 1999).

10. I am grateful to Justice Aniruddha Bose of the Calcutta High Court for confirming this information.

11. Nariaki Nakazato, *Neonationalist Mythology in Postwar Japan: Pal's Dissenting Judgment at the Tokyo War Crimes Tribunal* (Lanham, Md.: Lexington, 2016), 100.

12. The story of Pal's nomination to the tribunal has been thoroughly researched in Nakazato, *Neonationalist Mythology*, 3–28.

13. Ashis Nandy, "The Other Within: The Strange Case of Radhabinod Pal's Judgment of Culpability," *The Savage Freud and Other Essays on Possible and Retrievable Selves* (Princeton, N.J.: Princeton University Press, 1995), 53–80. Nandy interprets Pal's judgment in terms of a culturally inherited ethical world depicted in the Mahabharata in which both victor and vanquished were required to share the responsibility of originating a war. According to Nandy, Pal believed that "the West had to acknowledge that war-time Japan wanted to beat the West at its own game, that a significant part of Japanese imperialism was only a reflection of the West's disowned self." Nandy, "The Other Within," 79.

14. Nakazato, *Neonationalist Mythologies*.

15. Pal, *Dissentient Judgment*, 62; hereafter, page numbers will be cited parenthetically in the text.

16. Indeed, Bert Röling, the Dutch judge at Tokyo, later agreed that Hirota, the Japanese prime minister, was not guilty of aggressive war: "Hirota's foreign policy, if pursued, would have succeeded in expelling the European powers from Asia. It would have made Japan into one of the leading nations in the world. But what he did was not an international crime." B. V. A. Röling, *The Tokyo*

Trial and Beyond: Reflections of a Peacemonger, ed. Antonio Cassese (Cambridge, UK: Polity, 1993), 45.

17. Once again, Röling, speaking some thirty years later, agreed. Answering the question, "Would you say that there was an essential difference between the Germans accused in Nuremberg and the Japanese in Tokyo?" he said, "Oh yes! There was no question of similarity. The Japanese accused had no bad conscience at all! And maybe that was right, because the cruel people in the field were not our accused. Our accused were the leaders and they had never, at least as far as our evidence went, committed war crimes or ordered war crimes to be committed. The Nuremberg accused were quite a different story." Röling, *Tokyo Trial*, 46.

18. Röling, in *Tokyo Trial*, 84, also felt that the Allied bombing of Japanese cities with a view to causing such massive civilian deaths as to force Japan to surrender was a war crime:

> I sometimes had contact with Japanese students. The first thing they always asked was: "Are you morally entitled to sit in judgment over the leaders of Japan when the Allies have burned down all of its cities with sometimes, as in Tokyo, in one night, 100,000 deaths and which culminated in the destruction of Hiroshima and Nagasaki? Those were war crimes." I am strongly convinced that these bombings were war crimes. It was terrorizing the population with the purpose of making war painful beyond endurance so that the civilian population would urge the government to capitulate. It was terror warfare, "coercive warfare." And that is forbidden by the laws of war, for sure.

But to raise the question of war crimes committed by the Allies was ruled out by the tribunal's terms.

19. According to the Hiroshima newspaper *Chūkogu Shimbon*, November 4, 1952, quoted in Takeshi Nakajima, "Justice Pal (India)," in *Beyond Victor's Justice? The Tokyo War Crimes Trial Revisited*, ed. Yuki Tanaka, Tim McCormack, and Gerry Simpson (Leiden, Netherlands: Nijhoff, 2011), 140,

On seeing the memorial's inscription, "Let all the souls here rest in peace. For we shall not repeat the evil," Pal said as follows: "Obviously, the subject of 'we' is Japanese. I do not see clearly what 'the evil' means here. The souls being wished to rest here are the victims of the Atomic Bomb. It is clear to me that the bomb was not dropped by the Japanese and the hands of the bombers remain bloodstained. . . . If not repeating the mistake means not possessing weapons in the future, I think that is a very exemplary decision. If Japan wishes to possess military power again, that would be a defilement against the souls of the victims we have here in Hiroshima."

20. Nakazato, *Neonationalist Mythologies*, 173. Nakazato, 106, also tells us that in 1965 Pal expressly set out his views for the abolition of capital punishment in India.

21. Pal, *Dissentient Judgment*, 700. Notably, Justice Röling had a strikingly realist view of the political nature of the trial: "It was horrible that we went there for the purpose of vindicating the laws of war, and yet saw every day how the Allies had violated them dreadfully. But to claim that there should be a trial in which vanquished and victors should both be held in judgment, that's impossible. Tojo was right that in this respect, Tokyo was victor's justice only." Röling, *Tokyo Trial*, 87.

22. Pal, *Dissentient Judgment*, 700.

23. See, for example, Judith Shklar, *Legalism: Law, Politics, and Political Trials* (Cambridge, Mass.: Harvard University Press, 1986); Elizabeth S. Kopelman, "Ideology and International Law: The Dissent of the Indian Justice at the Tokyo War Crimes Trial," *New York University Journal of International Law and Politics* 23, no. 2 (1991): 373–444; and Neil Boister and Robert Cryer, *The Tokyo International Military Tribunal: A Reappraisal* (Oxford: Oxford University Press, 2008).

24. Pal, *Crimes*, 51; hereafter, page numbers will be cited parenthetically in the text.

25. For a reappraisal by international law scholars of the Bandung Declaration, see Luis Esteva, Michael Fakhri, and Vasuki Nesiah, eds., *Bandung, Global History, and International Law: Critical Pasts and Pending Futures* (Cambridge, UK: Cambridge University Press, 2017).

26. Tanisha M. Fazal, "Why States No Longer Declare War," *Security Studies* 21, no. 4 (2012): 557–93.

27. Marlise Simons, Rick Gladstone, and Carol Rosenberg, "International Court Abandons Afghanistan War Crimes Inquiry," *New York Times*, April 13, 2019.

28. For a critical discussion of an attempt on behalf of global civil society to charge the authorities of the U.S. government with waging an illegal war and violating human rights, see Ayça Çubukçu, *For the Love of Humanity: The World Tribunal on Iraq* (Philadelphia: University of Pennsylvania Press, 2018).

29. For a detailed critique, see Nakazato, *Neonationalist Mythologies.*

30. Johann Gottlieb Fichte, *Addresses to the German Nation*, ed. Isaac Nakhimovsky, Béla Kapossy and Keith Tribe (Indianapolis, Ind.: Hackett, 2013).

31. For a discussion of these two strands of interpretation of Fichte's addresses, see Arash Abizadeh, "Was Fichte an Ethnic Nationalist? On Cultural Nationalism and Its Double," *History of Political Thought* 26, no. 2 (2005): 234–59.

32. Johann Gottlieb Fichte, "Eighth Address: What a People, in the Higher Sense of the Word, Is; and What Love of One's Country Is," in *Addresses*, 95; hereafter, page numbers will be cited parenthetically in the text.

33. Johann Gottlieb Fichte, "Contents of the Thirteenth Address: Continuation of the Previous Observations," in *Addresses*, 158. The text of the "Thirteenth Address" was lost in the censor's office; Fichte reconstructed it from memory for publication.

34. Isaac Nakhimovsky, *The Closed Commercial State: Perpetual Peace and Commercial Society from Rousseau to Fichte* (Princeton, N.J.: Princeton University Press, 2011).

35. Fichte, "Contents of the Thirteenth Address," 173.

36. Étienne Balibar, "Fichte and the Internal Border: On *Addresses to the German Nation*," in *Masses, Classes, Ideas: Studies on Politics and Philosophy Before and After Marx*, trans. James Swenson (New York: Routledge, 1994), 61–84.

37. Partha Chatterjee, *Nationalist Thought and the Colonial World: A Derivative Discourse?* (London: Zed, 1986); Partha Chatterjee, *The Nation and Its Fragments: Colonial and Postcolonial Histories* (Princeton, N.J.: Princeton University Press, 1993).

2. The Cynicism of Power

1. Talal Asad, *Secular Translations: Nation-State, Modern Self, and Calculative Reason* (New York: Columbia University Press, 2018), 47, 134–44.

2. Michel Foucault, *"Society Must Be Defended": Lectures at the Collège de France, 1975–76*, trans. David Macey (New York: Picador, 2003).

3. Michel Foucault, *The Punitive Society: Lectures at the Collège de France 1972–73*, trans. Graham Burchell (New York: Palgrave Macmillan, 2015), 21–36.

4. Michel Foucault, *Discipline and Punish: The Birth of the Prison*, trans. Alan Sheridan (New York: Vintage, 1978).

5. Foucault, *"Society,"* 37.

6. *Oxford English Dictionary*, online ed. (accessed July 9, 2019), s.v. "race": "II. In extended use: a group or class of people, animals, or things, having some common feature or features: 6a. A set or class of people who share a characteristic attitude or other feature."

7. Foucault, *"Society,"* 50.

8. Foucault, *"Society,"* 98.

9. Foucault, *"Society,"* 103.

10. Edmund Burke, "Speech on Opening of Impeachment, 16 February 1788," in *The Writings and Speeches of Edmund Burke*, vol. 6, ed. P. J. Marshall (Oxford: Clarendon, 1991), 316–17.

11. Thomas Babington Macaulay, "Lord Clive," in *Macaulay's Critical and Historical Essays* (London: Dent, 1946), 1:479.

12. Immanuel Kant, "Perpetual Peace," in *On History*, trans. and ed. Lewis White Beck (Indianapolis, Ind.: Bobbs-Merrill, 1963), 85–136.

13. Foucault, *"Society,"* 134.

14. Foucault, *"Society,"* 142.

15. Foucault, *"Society,"* 142.

16. For my own examination of the logic of the balance of power system, see Partha Chatterjee, *Arms, Alliances and Stability: The Development of the Structure of International Politics* (New York: Wiley, 1975).

17. For my own examination of this aspect of sovereignty theory, see Partha Chatterjee, *The Black Hole of Empire: History of a Global Practice of Power* (Princeton, N.J.: Princeton University Press, 2012).

18. For an analysis of the policy of indirect rule, see Mahmood Mamdani, *Citizens and Subjects: Contemporary Africa and the Legacy of Late Colonialism* (Princeton, N.J.: Princeton University Press, 1996).

19. Antonio Gramsci, "The Revolution Against 'Capital,'" in *Selections from Political Writings (1910–1920)*, ed. Quintin Hoare, trans. John Matthews (London: Lawrence and Wishart, 1977), 34–37.

20. Antonio Gramsci, "Notebook 1," trans. Joseph Buttigieg, sec. 44, in *Prison Notebooks*, ed. Joseph Buttigieg (New York: Columbia University Press, 2011), 1:147.

21. Gramsci, "Notebook 1," sec. 44, 1:147.

22. Gramsci, "Notebook 1," sec. 44, 1:148. Gramsci's characterization of the historical significance of the Jacobins, and of Napoleon in the subsequent phase, largely follows Karl Marx and Friedrich Engels, *The Holy Family, or Critique of Critical Criticism: Against Bruno Bauer and Company*, trans. Richard Dixon and Clemens Dutt (1844; Moscow: Progress, 1975), 140–45, and Karl Marx, "The Eighteenth Brumaire of Louis Bonaparte," (1852) in Karl Marx, *Surveys from Exile*, trans. and ed. David Fernbach (Harmondsworth: Penguin, 1973), 143–249.

23. Gramsci, "Notebook 1," sec. 47, 1:153.

24. Gramsci, "Notebook 1," sec. 47, 1:156.

25. Gramsci's treatment of the ethical state is well explained in Peter D. Thomas, *The Gramscian Moment: Philosophy, Hegemony and Marxism* (Chicago: Haymarket, 2010), 180–82.

26. Antonio Gramsci, *Selections from the Prison Notebooks*, ed. and trans. Quintin Hoare and Geoffrey Nowell-Smith (New York: International, 1971), 119.

27. Gramsci, "Notebook 4," trans. Joseph Buttigieg, sec. 3, in *Prison Notebooks*, ed. Joseph Buttigieg (New York: Columbia University Press, 2011), 2:142.

28. Gramsci, "Notebook 4," sec. 49, 2:204–5.

29. This is argued in Timothy Mitchell, *Carbon Democracy: Political Power in the Age of Oil* (London: Verso, 2011), 66–85; and Joseph Massad, "Against Self-Determination," *Humanity Journal* 9, no. 2 (September 11, 2018).

30. William Beveridge, *Social Insurance and Allied Services: Report* (London: His Majesty's Stationery Office, 1942).

31. Beveridge, *Social Insurance*, 6–7.

32. Michel Foucault, *The Birth of Biopolitics: Lectures at the Collège de France, 1978–1979*, trans. Graham Burchell (New York: Picador, 2005), 216.

33. T. H. Marshall, "Citizenship and Social Class," in *Class, Citizenship and Social Development* (New York: Doubleday, 1965), 73–134.

34. Marshall, "Citizenship and Social Class," 76–77.

35. Marshall, "Citizenship and Social Class," 120–21.

36. Michel Foucault, *Security, Territory, Population: Lectures at the Collège de France, 1977–1978*, trans. Graham Burchell (New York: Picador, 2007), 63.

37. Foucault, *Security, Territory, Population*, 99.

38. Foucault, *The Birth of Biopolitics*, 296.

39. Marshall, "Citizenship and Social Class," 122–23.

40. Marshall, "Citizenship and Social Class," 124.

41. The main texts are Friedrich A. von Hayek, *Road to Serfdom* (1944; Chicago: University of Chicago Press, 1964); Milton Friedman, *Capitalism and Freedom* (Chicago: University of Chicago Press, 1962); and Gary Becker, *Human Capital: A Theoretical and Empirical*

Analysis with Special Reference to Education (Chicago: University of Chicago Press, 1983).

42. Foucault, *Birth of Biopolitics*, 207.

43. Karl Marx, *Capital*, trans. Ben Fowkes (London: Penguin, 1990), chap. 25, sec. 3, 1:781–94.

44. Marx, "The Eighteenth Brumaire."

45. Stanisława Przybyszewska, *The Danton Case*, act 5, scene 5, in *Two Plays*, trans. Boleslaw Taborski (Evanston, Ill.: Northwestern University Press, 1989), 199.

46. Émile Durkheim, "Preface to the Second Edition," in *Rules of Sociological Method*); 2nd ed., trans. W. W. Halls, ed. Steven Lukes (New York: Free Press, 1982), 34–46.

47. Ian Hacking, *The Taming of Chance* (Cambridge: Cambridge University Press, 1990); Alain Desrosieres, *The Politics of Large Numbers: A History of Statistical Reasoning*, trans. Camille Naish (Cambridge, Mass.: Harvard University Press, 1998).

48. Bernard E. Harcourt, *Against Prediction: Profiling, Policing and Punishing in an Actuarial Age* (Chicago: University of Chicago Press, 2007).

49. Asad, *Secular Translations*.

50. Richard H. Thaler, *Misbehaving: The Making of Behavioral Economics* (New York: Norton, 2015).

51. Abhijit V. Banerjee and Esther Duflo, *Poor Economics: A Radical Rethinking of the Way to Fight Global Poverty* (New York: Public Affairs, 2011).

52. Jerry Z. Muller, *The Tyranny of Metrics* (Princeton, N.J.: Princeton University Press, 2018).

53. Foucault, *Security, Territory, Population*, 43–44.

54. Alain Badiou, "Twenty-Four Notes on the Uses of the Word 'People,'" in *What Is a People?* ed. Bruno Bosteels and Kevin Olson, trans. Jody Gladding (New York: Columbia University Press, 2016), 24.

55. Judith Butler, "'We, the People': Thoughts on Freedom of Assembly," in Bosteels and Olson, eds., *What Is a People?*, 51.

56. Jacques Rancière, "The Populism That Is Not to Be Found," in Bosteels and Olson, eds., *What is a People?*, 102.

57. Georg Büchner, *Danton's Death*, act 1, scene 3, in *The Plays of Georg Büchner*, trans. Victor Price (London: Oxford University Press, 1971), 15.

3. "I Am the People"

1. For a useful account, see Pranab Bardhan, *The Political Economy of Development in India* (Oxford: Blackwell, 1984).

2. Ranajit Guha, *Dominance Without Hegemony: History and Power in Colonial India* (Cambridge, Mass.: Harvard University Press, 1997).

3. Partha Chatterjee, *The Politics of the Governed: Reflections on Popular Politics in Most of the World* (New York: Columbia University Press, 2004); Partha Chatterjee, *Lineages of Political Society: Studies in Postcolonial Democracy* (New York: Columbia University Press, 2011).

4. Sudipta Kaviraj, "An Outline of a Revisionist Theory of Modernity," *Archives européennes de sociologie* 46, no. 3 (2005): 497–526.

5. For a discussion of these arguments, see Partha Chatterjee, "Ambedkar's Theory of Minority Rights," in *The Radical in Ambedkar: Critical Reflections*, ed. Suraj Yengde and Anand Teltumbde (New Delhi: Penguin Random House, 2018), 107–33.

6. Kalyan Sanyal, *Rethinking Capitalist Development: Primitive Accumulation, Governmentality and Postcolonial Capitalism* (New York: Routledge, 2007).

7. Partha Chatterjee, "Land and the Political Management of Primitive Accumulation," in *The Land Question in India: State, Dispossession and Capitalist Transition*, ed. Anthony P. D'Costa and Achin Chakraborty (Oxford: Oxford University Press, 2017), 1–15.

8. Ernesto Laclau, *On Populist Reason* (London: Verso, 2005).

9. Ernesto Laclau, "Populism: What's in a Name?" in *Populism and the Mirror of Democracy*, ed. Francisco Panizza (London: Verso, 2005), 32–40.

10. Jan-Werner Müller, *What Is Populism?* (Philadelphia: University of Pennsylvania Press, 2016).

11. Pierre Rosanvallon, *Counter-democracy: Politics in an Age of Distrust* (Cambridge: Cambridge University Press, 2008), 273.

12. Nadia Urbinati, *Democracy Disfigured: Opinion, Truth and the People* (Cambridge, Mass.: Harvard University Press, 2014).

13. Steven Levitsky and Daniel Ziblatt, *How Democracies Die* (New York: Broadway, 2019).

14. David Runciman has a darker analysis, arguing that representative democracy may have outlived its relevance, but does not suggest how a form of government more appropriate for today's economic and technological conditions might be built. See David Runciman, *How Democracy Ends* (London: Profile, 2018).

15. M. Madhava Prasad, "The Republic of Babel: Language and Political Subjectivity in Free India," in *Theorizing the Present: Essays for Partha Chatterjee*, ed. Anjan Ghosh, Tapati Guha-Thakurta, and Janaki Nair (New Delhi: Oxford University Press, 2011), 65–81.

16. For a recounting of the period, see Gyan Prakash, *Emergency Chronicles: Indira Gandhi and Democracy's Turning Point* (Princeton, N.J.: Princeton University Press, 2018).

17. Sudipta Kaviraj, "A Critique of the Passive Revolution," *Economic and Political Weekly* 23, nos. 45–47 (1988): 2429–44.

18. M. S. S. Pandian, *Brahmin and Non-Brahmin: Genealogies of the Tamil Political Present* (Delhi: Permanent Black, 2007).

19. Pandian, *Brahmin and Non-Brahmin*, 196–205.

20. Narendra Subramanian, *Ethnicity and Populist Mobilization: Political Parties, Citizens and Democracy in South India* (New Delhi: Oxford University Press, 1999), 36.

21. Subramanian, *Ethnicity*, 73–78.

22. Pandian, *Brahmin and Non-Brahmin*, 236–44.

23. M. Madhava Prasad, *Cine-politics: Film Stars and Political Existence in South India* (Hyderabad, India: Orient Blackswan, 2014); hereafter, page numbers will be cited parenthetically in the text.

24. Homi K. Bhabha has very usefully pointed out in a personal communication that the populist leader "embodies the myth and magic (the cinematic mix) of being at once survivor and the savior of 'the people' (melodrama) and *yet* [is] *beyond its reach*. This idea of the populist leader being 'beyond the reach,' and yet at

'eye-level,' seems to me crucially important." I am grateful to him for suggesting this point.

25. See the discussion of praise in Bernard Bate, *Tamil Oratory and the Dravidian Aesthetic: Democratic Practice in South India* (New York: Columbia University Press, 2009), 38–67.

26. Prasad, *Cine-Politics*, 40.

27. Prasad, *Cine-Politics*, 56.

28. The most systematic study is Ravi Vasudevan, *The Melodramatic Public: Film Form and Spectatorship in Indian Cinema* (Ranikhet, India: Permanent Black, 2010).

29. This point has been well argued in Gyanendra Pandey, ed., *Hindus and Others: The Question of Identity in India Today* (New York: Viking, 1993).

30. I have made this argument at greater length in Partha Chatterjee, "A Relativist View of the Indian Nation," in *Rethinking Social Justice: Essays in Honour of M. S. S. Pandian*, ed. S. Anandhi, Karthick Ram Manoharan, M. Vijayabaskar, and A. Kalaiyarasan (New Delhi: Orient Blackswan, 2019).

31. Ajay Gudavarthy, *India After Modi: Populism and the Right* (New Delhi: Bloomsbury, 2018).

32. Richard Tuck, *The Sleeping Sovereign: The Invention of Modern Democracy* (Cambridge: Cambridge University Press, 2015).

33. Tuck, *Sleeping Sovereign*, 241.

34. William H. Riker, *Liberalism Against Populism: A Confrontation Between the Theory of Democracy and the Theory of Social Choice* (Prospect Heights, Ill.: Waveland, 1982), 233–53.

35. Carl Sandburg, "I Am the People, the Mob," in *The Complete Poems of Carl Sandburg* (New York: Houghton Mifflin Harcourt, 2003), 71.

Afterword: The Optimism of the Intellect

1. Carl Schmitt, *Political Theology: Four Chapters on the Concept of Sovereignty*, trans. George Schwab (1922; Chicago: University of Chicago Press, 1985), 30.

2. Schmitt, *Political Theology*, 31.

3. Jeremy Harding, "Among the Gilets Jaunes," *London Review of Books* 41, no. 6 (2019): 3–11.

4. A widely discussed demonstration of the growing inequality in Western countries is Thomas Piketty, *Capital in the Twenty-First Century* (Cambridge, Mass.: Harvard University Press, 2017).

5. Chantal Mouffe, *For a Left Populism* (London: Verso, 2018).

6. Even though she does not argue for a left-wing variety of populism, Wendy Brown, after criticizing the pervasive depoliticization brought about by neoliberal rationality, also pleads for a return to the ancient Greek or civic republican ideal of *Homo politicus. Undoing the Demos: Neoliberalism's Stealth Revolution* (New York: Zone Books, 2015).

7. Mouffe, *Left Populism*, 49–50.

8. Ben S. Bernanke, *The Courage to Act: A Memoir of a Crisis and Its Aftermath* (New York: Norton, 2015).

9. Adam Tooze, *Crashed: How a Decade of Financial Crises Changed the World* (New York: Viking, 2018), 13; hereafter, page numbers will be cited parenthetically in the text.

10. Jean-Claude Juncker, quoted in Tooze, *Crashed*, 382.

11. Tooze, *Crashed*, 614.

12. Thomas Blom Hansen, "Democracy Against the Law: Reflections on India's Illiberal Democracy," in *Majoritarian State: How Hindu Nationalism Is Changing India*, ed. Angana P. Chatterjee, Thomas Blom Hansen, and Christophe Jaffrelot (London: Hurst, 2019).

13. Siva Vaidhyanathan, *Antisocial Media: How Facebook Disconnects Us and Undermines Democracy* (New York: Oxford University Press, 2018), 14–15.

14. Peter Thiel, quoted in Tooze, *Crashed*, 461–62.

BIBLIOGRAPHY

Abizadeh, Arash. "Was Fichte an Ethnic Nationalist? On Cultural Nationalism and Its Double." *History of Political Thought* 26, no. 2 (2005): 234–59.

Asad, Talal. *Secular Translations: Nation-State, Modern Self, and Calculative Reason.* New York: Columbia University Press, 2018.

Balibar, Étienne. *Masses, Classes, Ideas: Studies on Politics and Philosophy Before and After Marx.* Translated by James Swenson. New York: Routledge, 1994.

Banerjee, Abhijit V., and Esther Duflo. *Poor Economics: A Radical Rethinking of the Way to Fight Global Poverty.* New York: Public Affairs, 2011.

Bardhan, Pranab. *The Political Economy of Development in India.* Oxford: Blackwell, 1984.

Bate, Bernard. *Tamil Oratory and the Dravidian Aesthetic: Democratic Practice in South India.* New York: Columbia University Press, 2009.

Becker, Gary. *Human Capital: A Theoretical and Empirical Analysis with Special Reference to Education.* Chicago: University of Chicago Press, 1983.

Benedict, Ruth. *The Chrysanthemum and the Sword: Patterns of Japanese Culture.* Boston: Houghton Mifflin, 2006.

Bernanke, Ben S. *The Courage to Act: A Memoir of a Crisis and Its Aftermath.* New York: Norton, 2015.

Beveridge, William. *Social Insurance and Allied Services: Report*. London: His Majesty's Stationery Office, 1942.

Boister, Neil, and Robert Cryer. *The Tokyo International Military Tribunal: A Reappraisal*. Oxford: Oxford University Press, 2008.

Bosteels, Bruno, and Kevin Olson, eds. *What Is a People?* Translated by Jody Gladding. New York: Columbia University Press, 2016.

Brown, Wendy. *Undoing the Demos: Neoliberalism's Stealth Revolution*. New York: Zone Books, 2015.

Büchner, Georg. *The Plays of Georg Büchner*. Translated by Victor Price. London: Oxford University Press, 1971.

Burke, Edmund. *The Writings and Speeches of Edmund Burke*. Vol. 6. Edited by P. J. Marshall. Oxford: Clarendon Press, 1991.

Caffrey, Margaret M. *Ruth Benedict: Stranger in This Land*. Austin: University of Texas Press, 1989.

Chatterjee, Partha. "Ambedkar's Theory of Minority Rights." In *The Radical in Ambedkar: Critical Reflections*, edited by Suraj Yengde and Anand Teltumbde, 107–33. New Delhi: Penguin Random House, 2018.

——. *Arms, Alliances and Stability: The Development of the Structure of International Politics*. New York: Wiley, 1975.

——. *The Black Hole of Empire: History of a Global Practice of Power*. Princeton, N.J.: Princeton University Press, 2012.

——. "Land and the Political Management of Primitive Accumulation." In *The Land Question in India: State, Dispossession and Capitalist Transition*, edited by Anthony P. D'Costa and Achin Chakraborty, 1–15. Oxford: Oxford University Press, 2017.

——. *Lineages of Political Society: Studies in Postcolonial Democracy*. New York: Columbia University Press, 2011.

——. *The Nation and Its Fragments: Colonial and Postcolonial Histories*. Princeton, N.J.: Princeton University Press, 1993.

——. *Nationalist Thought and the Colonial World: A Derivative Discourse?* London: Zed, 1986.

——. *The Politics of the Governed: Reflections on Popular Politics in Most of the World*. New York: Columbia University Press, 2004.

——. "A Relativist View of the Indian Nation." In *Rethinking Social Justice: Essays in Honour of M. S. S. Pandian*, edited by S. Anandhi, Karthick Ram Manoharan, M. Vijayabaskar, and A. Kalaiyarasan. New Delhi: Orient Blackswan, 2019.

Çubukçu, Ayça. *For the Love of Humanity: The World Tribunal on Iraq.* Philadelphia: University of Pennsylvania Press, 2018.

Desrosieres, Alain. *The Politics of Large Numbers: A History of Statistical Reasoning.* Translated by Camille Naish. Cambridge, Mass.: Harvard University Press, 1998.

Dumont, Louis. *From Mandeville to Marx: The Genesis and Triumph of Economic Ideology.* Chicago: University of Chicago Press, 1977.

——. *Homo Hierarchicus: The Caste System and Its Implications.* Chicago: University of Chicago Press, 1970.

Durkheim, Émile. *Rules of Sociological Method.* Translated by W. W. Halls. Edited by Steven Lukes. New York: Free Press, 1982.

Esteva, Luis, Michael Fakhri, and Vasuki Nesiah, eds. *Bandung, Global History, and International Law: Critical Pasts and Pending Futures.* Cambridge: Cambridge University Press, 2017.

Fazal, Tanisha M. "Why States No Longer Declare War." *Security Studies* 21, no. 4 (2012): 557–93.

Fichte, Johann Gottlieb. *Addresses to the German Nation.* Edited by Isaac Nakhimovsky, Béla Kapossy, and Keith Tribe. Indianapolis, Ind.: Hackett, 2013.

Foucault, Michel. *The Birth of Biopolitics: Lectures at the Collège de France, 1978–1979.* Translated by Graham Burchell. New York: Picador, 2005.

——. *Discipline and Punish: The Birth of the Prison.* Translated by Alan Sheridan. New York: Vintage, 1978.

——. *The Punitive Society: Lectures at the Collège de France, 1972–73.* Translated by Graham Burchell. New York: Palgrave Macmillan, 2015.

——. *Security, Territory, Population: Lectures at the Collège de France, 1977–1978.* Translated by Graham Burchell. New York: Picador, 2007.

——. *"Society Must Be Defended": Lectures at the Collège de France, 1975–76.* Translated by David Macey. New York: Picador, 2003.

Friedman, Milton. *Capitalism and Freedom.* Chicago: University of Chicago Press, 1962.

Gramsci, Antonio. *Prison Notebooks.* 3 vols. Edited by Joseph Buttigieg. New York: Columbia University Press, 2011.

——. *Selections from Political Writings (1910–1920).* Edited by Quintin Hoare. Translated by John Matthews. London: Lawrence and Wishart, 1977.

——. *Selections from the Prison Notebooks.* Edited and translated by Quintin Hoare and Geoffrey Nowell-Smith. New York: International, 1971.

Gudavarthy, Ajay. *India After Modi: Populism and the Right.* New Delhi: Bloomsbury, 2018.

Guha, Ranajit. *Dominance Without Hegemony: History and Power in Colonial India.* Cambridge, Mass.: Harvard University Press, 1997.

Hacking, Ian. *The Taming of Chance.* Cambridge: Cambridge University Press, 1990.

Hansen, Thomas Blom. "Democracy Against the Law: Reflections on India's Illiberal Democracy." In *Majoritarian State: How Hindu Nationalism Is Changing India*, edited by Angana P. Chatterjee, Thomas Blom Hansen, and Christophe Jaffrelot. London: Hurst, 2019.

Harcourt, Bernard E. *Against Prediction: Profiling, Policing and Punishing in an Actuarial Age.* Chicago: University of Chicago Press, 2007.

Harding, Jeremy. "Among the Gilets Jaunes." *London Review of Books* 41, no. 6 (2019): 3–11.

Hayek, Friedrich A. von. *Road to Serfdom.* Chicago: University of Chicago Press, 1964.

Kant, Immanuel. *On History.* Edited by Lewis White Beck. Indianapolis, Ind.: Bobbs-Merrill, 1963.

Kaviraj, Sudipta. "A Critique of the Passive Revolution." *Economic and Political Weekly* 23, nos. 45–47 (1988): 2429–44.

——. "An Outline of a Revisionist Theory of Modernity." *Archives européennes de sociologie* 46, no. 3 (2005): 497–526.

Kopelman, Elizabeth S. "Ideology and International Law: The Dissent of the Indian Justice at the Tokyo War Crimes Trial." *New*

York University Journal of International Law and Politics 23, no. 2 (1991): 373–444.

Laclau, Ernesto. *On Populist Reason.* London: Verso, 2005.

——. "Populism: What's in a Name?" In *Populism and the Mirror of Democracy,* ed. Francisco Panizza, 32–40. London: Verso, 2005.

Levitsky, Steven, and Daniel Ziblatt. *How Democracies Die.* New York: Broadway, 2019.

Macaulay, Thomas Babington. *Macaulay's Critical and Historical Essays.* Vol. 1. London: Dent, 1946.

Mamdani, Mahmood. *Citizens and Subjects: Contemporary Africa and the Legacy of Late Colonialism.* Princeton, N.J.: Princeton University Press, 1996.

Marshall, T. H. *Class, Citizenship and Social Development.* New York: Doubleday, 1965.

Marx, Karl. *Capital.* Vol. 1. Translated by Ben Fowkes. London: Penguin, 1990.

——. "The Eighteenth Brumaire of Louis Bonaparte." In *Karl Marx, Surveys from Exile,* translated and edited by David Fernbach, 143–249. Harmondsworth: Penguin, 1973.

Marx, Karl, and Friedrich Engels. *The Holy Family, or Critique of Critical Criticism: Against Bruno Bauer and Company.* Translated by Richard Dixon and Clemens Dutt. Moscow: Progress, 1975.

Massad, Joseph. "Against Self-Determination." *Humanity Journal* 9, no. 2 (2018).

Mead, Margaret. *Ruth Benedict.* New York: Columbia University Press, 1972.

Minear, Richard H. *Victors' Justice: The Tokyo War Crimes Trial.* Princeton, N.J.: Princeton University Press, 1971.

Mitchell, Timothy. *Carbon Democracy: Political Power in the Age of Oil.* London: Verso, 2011.

Müller, Jan-Werner. *What Is Populism?* Philadelphia: University of Pennsylvania Press, 2016.

Muller, Jerry Z. *The Tyranny of Metrics.* Princeton, N.J.: Princeton University Press, 2018.

Modell, Judith Schachter. *Ruth Benedict: Patterns of a Life.* Philadelphia: University of Pennsylvania Press, 1984.

Mouffe, Chantal. *For a Left Populism.* London: Verso, 2018.

Mukerjee, Madhusree. *Churchill's Secret War: The British Empire and the Ravaging of India During World War II.* Boston: Basic Books, 2011.

Nakajima, Takeshi. "Justice Pal (India)." In *Beyond Victor's Justice? The Tokyo War Crimes Trial Revisited*, edited by Yuki Tanaka, Tim McCormack, and Gerry Simpson, 127–44. Leiden, Netherlands: Nijhoff, 2011.

Nakazato, Nariaki. *Neonationalist Mythology in Postwar Japan: Pal's Dissenting Judgment at the Tokyo War Crimes Tribunal.* Lanham, Md.: Lexington, 2016.

Nakhimovsky, Isaac. *The Closed Commercial State: Perpetual Peace and Commercial Society from Rousseau to Fichte.* Princeton, N.J.: Princeton University Press, 2011.

Nandy, Ashis. *The Savage Freud and Other Essays on Possible and Retrievable Selves.* Princeton, N.J.: Princeton University Press, 1995.

Pal, Radhabinod. *Crimes in International Relations.* Calcutta: University of Calcutta, 1955.

——. *International Military Tribunal for the Far East: Dissentient Judgment of Justice Pal.* Tokyo: Kokusho-Kankokai, 1999.

Pandey, Gyanendra, ed. *Hindus and Others: The Question of Identity in India Today.* New York: Viking, 1993.

Pandian, M. S. S. *Brahmin and Non-Brahmin: Genealogies of the Tamil Political Present.* Delhi: Permanent Black, 2007.

Piketty, Thomas. *Capital in the Twenty-First Century.* Cambridge, Mass.: Harvard University Press, 2017.

Prakash, Gyan. *Emergency Chronicles: Indira Gandhi and Democracy's Turning Point.* Princeton, N.J.: Princeton University Press, 2018.

Prasad, M. Madhava. *Cine-politics: Film Stars and Political Existence in South India.* Hyderabad, India: Orient Blackswan, 2014.

——. "The Republic of Babel: Language and Political Subjectivity in Free India." In *Theorizing the Present: Essays for Partha Chatterjee*, edited by Anjan Ghosh, Tapati Guha-Thakurta and Janaki Nair, 65–81. New Delhi: Oxford University Press, 2011.

Przybyszewska, Stanisława. *Two Plays.* Translated by Bolesław Taborski. Evanston, Ill.: Northwestern University Press, 1989.

Riker, William H. *Liberalism Against Populism: A Confrontation Between the Theory of Democracy and the Theory of Social Choice.* Prospect Heights, Ill.: Waveland, 1982.

Röling, B. V. A. *The Tokyo Trial and Beyond: Reflections of a Peacemonger.* Edited by Antonio Cassese. Cambridge: Polity, 1993.

Rosanvallon, Pierre. *Counter-democracy: Politics in an Age of Distrust.* Cambridge: Cambridge University Press, 2008.

Runciman, David. *How Democracy Ends.* London: Profile, 2018.

Sandburg, Carl. *The Complete Poems of Carl Sandburg.* New York: Houghton Mifflin Harcourt, 2003.

Sanyal, Kalyan. *Rethinking Capitalist Development: Primitive Accumulation, Governmentality and Postcolonial Capitalism.* New York: Routledge, 2007.

Schmitt, Carl. *Political Theology: Four Chapters on the Concept of Sovereignty.* Translated by George Schwab. Chicago: University of Chicago Press, 1985.

Shklar, Judith. *Legalism: Law, Politics, and Political Trials.* Cambridge, Mass.: Harvard University Press, 1986.

Simons, Marlise, Rick Gladstone, and Carol Rosenberg. "International Court Abandons Afghanistan War Crimes Inquiry." *New York Times,* April 13, 2019.

Subramanian, Narendra. *Ethnicity and Populist Mobilization: Political Parties, Citizens and Democracy in South India.* New Delhi: Oxford University Press, 1999.

Thaler, Richard H. *Misbehaving: The Making of Behavioral Economics.* New York: Norton, 2015.

Thomas, Peter D. *The Gramscian Moment: Philosophy, Hegemony and Marxism.* Chicago: Haymarket, 2010.

Tooze, Adam. *Crashed: How a Decade of Financial Crises Changed the World.* New York: Viking, 2018.

Tuck, Richard. *The Sleeping Sovereign: The Invention of Modern Democracy.* Cambridge: Cambridge University Press, 2015.

Urbinati, Nadia. *Democracy Disfigured: Opinion, Truth and the People.* Cambridge, Mass.: Harvard University Press, 2014.

Vaidhyanathan, Siva. *Antisocial Media: How Facebook Disconnects Us and Undermines Democracy.* New York: Oxford University Press, 2018.

Vasudevan, Ravi. *The Melodramatic Public: Film Form and Spectatorship in Indian Cinema.* Ranikhet, India: Permanent Black, 2010.

INDEX